IMAGES
of Rail

BUILDING GRAND
CENTRAL TERMINAL

The intense 48-foot sculptural masterpiece by Frenchman Jules-Félix Coutan (1848–1939) and the world's largest stained-glass clock, with a 13-foot circumference, from the studio of Louis Comfort Tiffany (1848–1933), form the pinnacle of Grand Central Terminal. The sculpture, titled the *Glory of Commerce*, shows Hercules, Minerva, and Mercury (the group is called Transportation). A model of the sculpture was produced in Paris from 1911 to 1914 in the Beaux-Arts style and then carved in the Long Island City workshop of William Bradley and Son. (Photograph by Carol M. Highsmith, courtesy of the Carol M. Highsmith Archive in the Library of Congress Prints and Photographs Division.)

ON THE COVER: The massive building project is under way in this image dated July 13, 1907. The steel structure of Grand Central Post Office, on the left, will be attached to the east facade of Grand Central Terminal. Grand Central Station, completed seven years earlier, and Grand Central Depot's 19th-century European-styled train shed are visible on the right. Both will be razed. In the foreground, workers maneuver steam-powered cranes, newly electrified trains, and other equipment in their excavation of Bite No. 2, the second section of the new subterranean railyard. This photograph was taken by a New York Central & Hudson River Railroad (NYCHRR) photographer. (Courtesy of the NYCHRR Archives in the New York Public Library Irma and Paul Milstein Division of United States History, Local History, and Genealogy.)

IMAGES
of Rail

BUILDING GRAND
CENTRAL TERMINAL

Gregory Bilotto and Frank DiLorenzo
Foreword by James L. Sedore Jr.

ARCADIA
PUBLISHING

Published by Arcadia Publishing
Charleston, South Carolina

Printed in the United States of America

Library of Congress Control Number: 2016958622

For all general information, please contact Arcadia Publishing:
Telephone 843-853-2070
Fax 843-853-0044
E-mail sales@arcadiapublishing.com
For customer service and orders:
Toll-Free 1-888-313-2665

Visit us on the Internet at www.arcadiapublishing.com

The authors wish to memorialize those souls that perished in Manhattan on January 8, 1902, during Park Avenue's railroad tunnel collision. In the shameful absence of any commemoration or monument to the victims, this book is dedicated in their memory. It is the hope that the future will bring a formal memorial, to be erected at the crash site, Park Avenue and East Fifty-Sixth Street.

CONTENTS

FOREWORD

For over a century, an immense train terminal has dominated the landscape of Midtown Manhattan, providing essential links to transport and commerce. The structure, Grand Central Terminal, as well as the earlier phases, was the lucrative realization of one Gilded Age family and its patriarch, Cornelius Vanderbilt. The terminal, in its existing structure, was completed in 1913 and revolutionized railroad transport in the city of New York. Today, Grand Central Terminal remains even more vital than on opening day, with annual usage growing exponentially and its importance for both movements of people and capital almost incalculable. Paramount to these other values is the famous icon that the terminal has become to New York City and the world: an image immediately recognizable and treasured.

It is my true pleasure to introduce *Building Grand Central Terminal*, an insightful work with many images either never before published or long forgotten, written by Gregory Bilotto and Frank DiLorenzo. The book begins with an introduction on the earlier building phases and continues to the construction of the existing Grand Central Terminal. While most other great cities erected ornamental cast-iron train sheds, the city of New York was able to boast the greatest train terminal in the world. The authors have truly captured the unique history and significance of this impressive terminal as they continue the story beyond its construction and opening into the war years and later depreciation. The book concludes with the terminal's revival and modern use. Its exciting images and informative writing present a fascinating narration for both expert and enthusiast alike.

Both authors are known to me through their dedication to the Mount Beacon Incline Railway Restoration Society, a nonprofit organization dedicated to the historical and environmental preservation of the lost Mount Beacon Incline Railway and surrounding land. Frank is the project engineer, and we both serve as members of the board, while Gregory has authored *Along the Mount Beacon Incline Railway* (Arcadia 2015), documenting its history. As both the former chairman of the Metro-North Railroad Committee of the Metropolitan Transportation Authority's governing board and the representative of Dutchess County to the authority, it is with great pride that I can introduce this work, which illuminates the storied history of the crown jewel in New York's railroad network.

—James L. Sedore Jr.

Acknowledgments

The authors wish to express their gratitude for the advice, assistance, and generosity of Patricia Favata, Paul and Robert Gould, James L. Sedore Jr., Michael A. Vitiello, and, especially, title manager Henry Clougherty.

Our appreciation is also expressed to the following institutions and collections that have provided images for the publication of this book: the Robert N. Dennis Collection in the New York Public Library (NYPL) Miriam and Ira D. Wallach Division of Art, Prints, and Photographs; New York Central & Hudson River Railroad (NYCHRR) Archives in the NYPL Irma and Paul Milstein Division of US History, Local History, and Genealogy; and other NYPL collections and archives; Archives of the New York Railroad Enthusiasts in the Frederick Ely Williamson Library at Grand Central Terminal; Staten Island Museum at Snug Harbor; John Fleming Gould Collection in the Bethlehem Art Gallery; Bain Collection, Detroit Publishing Company Collection; and numerous other collections and archives in the Library of Congress (LOC) Division of Prints and Photographs.

Finally, the author Gregory Bilotto wishes to thank his parents, Sandra and Gerard, for their continued support and assistance throughout the entire research and writing process. They were a constant source of strength during a long and arduous period of work—especially at the Rhinebeck railroad station before departure for London. The author Frank DiLorenzo wishes to thank his wife, Nancy, a dedicated partner and collaborator through many adventures.

INTRODUCTION

It was a cold Wednesday morning, and snow was falling a few days after the New Year. Passengers boarded a suburban train arriving at the railroad station in White Plains. Beforehand in New Rochelle, passengers entered two rear carriages of train No. 223, originating from Norwalk, Connecticut. Both trains terminated at Grand Central Station via Park Avenue's railroad tunnel. It was January 8, 1902. On this day, unsafe conditions in the tunnel, although a daily occurrence, would produce fatal consequences. At 8:02 a.m., train No. 223 stopped in the tunnel awaiting entry to Grand Central Station during morning congestion. Meanwhile, the White Plains train passing several warning signals continued on the same track and subsequently impacted the two rear carriages of train No. 223. In the crash and aftermath, 17 persons perished and 36 were injured; nearly all were from New Rochelle. The macabre scene left the deceased strewn throughout the two crushed carriages and the tunnel. It was reported that three men in their attempt to escape the wreckage were found hanging from a carriage window, burned alive from intense steam. Another trapped passenger, Amanda Hungerford Howard (b. 1864), survived the crash only to be killed from escaping steam. According to 36-year-old Bronx motorman John Martin Wisker (1865–1909), steam, smoke, and cinder blocked his view of the warning signals and train No. 223.

The deadly crash had a resounding impact, and after public reaction to the accident demanded safety improvements, the board of directors for NYCHRR approved construction of a massive new terminal and subterranean railyard with a network of tunnels. Work on the project was to commence on August 17, 1903. As a direct result of the tunnel crash, on May 7, 1903, the New York State Legislature voted and approved a bill to prohibit all steam locomotives in New York County after June 30, 1908. Conversion to the electrification process began with the first electric-powered train trial at the High Bridge in Bronx County, which terminated at Grand Central Station on September 30, 1906. Converted before the required date, the trains utilized electric power until reaching Croton-Harmon and North White Plains stations. A steam-powered locomotive completed the journey north. It would not be until the 1923 Kaufman Electrification Act from Assemblyman Victor R. Kaufman that the New York State Legislature would mandate all train lines in New York City, both passenger and freight, be electrified. Before the 1902 rail collision and resulting legislation, the power of the Vanderbilt family's Gilded Age monopoly over railroad travel through the NYCHRR hindered implementation of any major safety changes or remedies to the polluted and dangerous environment in Grand Central Station.

Gilded Age America created a climate of soaring profits, enormous personal wealth, powerful monopolies, and controlling familial dynasties, while leaving incredible poverty, exploitation, and disenfranchisement in its wake. Nevertheless, during this period (1870s–early 1900s), enormous skyscrapers were erected, engineering marvels realized, and technological innovations materialized, from the RMS *Titanic* to the Fuller (Flatiron) Building and from the Otis electric elevator to riveted steel. It was also during this age that the new Grand Central Terminal, as it exists today, emerged through the thin gold lining of corruption, deprivation, and greed—a hypocrisy characterized by Mark Twain (1835–1910) and Charles Dudley Warner (1829–1900) in their novel *The Gilded Age: A Tale of Today*, published in 1873. It was accepted that the 1902 tunnel collision and succeeding legislation together formed the catalyst for action toward safety improvements and the ultimate creation of the terminal. It was, however, the public announcement from the rival railroad company on January 22, 1902, with the intention to construct Pennsylvania Station in Manhattan that aroused reaction motivating any real improvement.

The NYCHRR, managed through the Vanderbilt-controlled board of directors, had monopolized rail travel in New York County, and with its primary competitor, the Pennsylvania Railroad, now building a mammoth Midtown station in the Beaux-Arts style, the loss to income and exclusive control of rail transport became a reality. The board of directors once included the powerful titans William Kissam Vanderbilt (1849–1920) and Cornelius Vanderbilt II (1843–1899), both grandsons of Cornelius Vanderbilt (1794–1877), along with William Rockefeller (1841–1922), John Pierpont Morgan (1837–1913), William Fargo (1818–1881), and others. The board of directors in 1903, realizing the threat from the Pennsylvania Railroad, accepted the proposed plans for a new terminal. These plans came from visionary William John Wilgus (1865–1949), chief civil engineer of the NYCHRR. The approved changes called for a radically distinctive train terminal, which considered all of the flaws, safety concerns, and other issues from the site's earlier structures, Grand Central Depot (1871) and Grand Central Station (1900). The estimated $35,000,000 cost of the new terminal would be recovered through the sale of air rights, an ingenious idea from the chief engineer. This would allow high-rise buildings to be constructed over a subterranean railyard. Together, the industrialists on the board of directors accumulated massive wealth through collusion during the construction process, increased rail travel after completion, the sale of air rights, and development interests.

Grand Central Terminal opened with great fanfare at the stroke of midnight on February 2, 1913. A crowd of over 150,000 passed through on that first day, overlooking the railroad's scandalous and corrupt history. Nonetheless, it truly was a magnificent structure with many innovations and the latest modern conveniences, surpassing all other comparable stations worldwide, from London to Paris and beyond. The elegant terminal featured rooms for dining, shoeshine, telephones, and waiting, as well as a barbershop. All rooms were served with maids and attendants. The ornamental Guastavino tiles supported elongated vaults in the Oyster Bar and throughout the terminal. While delighting in the finest seafood and other delectable offerings, diners in the Oyster Bar sat among tropical plants and Persian carpets and below chandeliers and Rafael Guastavino's sublime tiling. Careful attention was given to the many features influenced by the Beaux-Arts style. French styles and monuments, favored by the Vanderbilts and especially Whitney Warren (1864–1943), one of the four architects that collectively designed Grand Central Terminal, are recognizable throughout its halls and rooms and in the ornate details. The acorn and oak leaves, heraldic symbols of the Vanderbilt family since the third generation, were emblazoned above every passage, precipice, and staircase of the terminal. Gone were the steam, smoke, cinder, problems of congestion, limited space, poor efficiency, and major safety issues.

It is the intention of this book to illustrate the history of Grand Central Terminal, the world's greatest railroad terminal, through the site's earlier structures, difficulties, and an era of greed and corruption leading to its creation. The story continues beyond the opening of the terminal into the world wars and its eventual decline and near demise with the dominance of the motorcar. Finally, the renaissance and renovation of the terminal leading to the modern day will be discussed, including the recent construction under way to erect an enormous skyscraper at One Vanderbilt Avenue, with new subterranean rail tunnels connecting to the terminal. Through this lens, an overlooked view of the terminal's history will be presented, expressed through many heretofore unseen and long-forgotten images. Perhaps the most profound concept about Grand Central Terminal is that the structure remains in perpetual motion, much like the people passing daily. The site has shifted and been transformed since the 19th century, leading to the current 1913-built terminal, which metamorphosed over the last 100 years—its prominent role having flourished, faded, and risen again, with only a singular function remaining constant: travel. The future remains positive for Grand Central Terminal, especially with increased automotive congestion and pollution on a massive scale, and the current trend is indicative of the railroad's augmented growth and long-term sustainability as the benefits of mass transportation become even more apparent.

The imposing mansion built on Ochre Point Avenue in Newport, Rhode Island, and known as the Breakers was designed for Cornelius Vanderbilt II in the Italian Renaissance style. Work on the house began in 1893 and was completed in 1895. The summer home was constructed on the cliffs overlooking the Atlantic Ocean and boasts five floors and 70 rooms, totalling 125,339 square feet. The house—designed by the talented architect Richard Morris Hunt (1827–1895), a Vanderbilt favorite, and with interiors by Jules Allard et Fils—was in use a few weeks during the summer season and remained shuttered throughout the rest of the year. It is the quintessential example of the splendor, opulence, and excess characteristic of Gilded Age America. Shown is the rear, or ocean side, of the home in 2014. (Photograph by Gregory Bilotto.)

One

MIDTOWN MANHATTAN AND THE COMMODORE

Cornelius Vanderbilt was born in Port Richmond, Richmond County (Staten Island), New York. His family farmed and ran a modest ferry as the poor descendants of a 17th-century indentured servant from Utrecht, the Netherlands. Cornelius Vanderbilt would initiate his own ferry company between the Staten and Manhattan Islands in 1810, eventually learning business acumen and legal matters. These skills would elevate him to great wealth through the formation of his shipping empire and giant NYCHRR. It was through the NYCHRR, however, that he would radically transform Manhattan and control rail travel throughout the Northeast, creating a monopoly via the acquisition and consolidation of numerous railroad companies. The association with the title *commodore* originated with his fellow boatmen during his youth. An alternative association stemmed from his control of shipping between both coasts of the United States, as dubbed by the American public in the 1860s. Epithets aside, transportation was the most important and lucrative industry in the 19th century and Cornelius Vanderbilt was king.

Development in New York County during the 19th century essentially ended at Forty-Second Street. Farther north, the island had a scattered population living on farms within the bounds of the natural terrain. A study of stereoscopic views showing the 1848-built High Bridge in Bronx County reveals sparse settlement along the Harlem River. (A stereoscopic view is a card with two photographs showing the left-eye and right-eye views of an identical scene. When viewed through a stereoscope, a three-dimensional image is projected.) These buildings would later give way to manicured parkland as routine visitors became more common, spurred by growth initiated with Grand Central Depot's construction. Further development in succeeding years would dramatically alter Manhattan's terrain. This process would subsequently be mimicked in Bronx County, but to a lesser extent. The shift in the natural terrain entailed the pacification of the land, including rock outcroppings, forests, and inshore bodies of water, creating mostly a plane topography for building—basically, all major obstacles were removed. Only a few areas survived the cull and exist today, providing a glimpse into the natural terrain of Manhattan Island, namely Central and Riverside Parks.

From the studio of renowned American Civil War photographer Mathew Brady (1822–1896) comes a head-and-shoulders portrait of Cornelius Vanderbilt made between 1844 and 1860. The middle-aged railroad tycoon is shown in puritanical simplicity, quite different from later Vanderbilt generations. The portrait was produced on a gold-toned half-plate daguerreotype, a very expensive photographic process developed in 1839 by Frenchman Louis-Jacques-Mandé Daguerre (1787–1851). The daguerreotype was restored by Michel Vuijlsteke. (Courtesy of the Daguerreotype Collection in the Library of Congress Prints and Photographs Division.)

The Hudson River School painter Jasper Francis Cropsey (1823–1900) has preserved 1895 life on the Vanderbilt estate in Richmond County, New York. The tranquil scenery of the farm with planted fields was a stark contrast to Gilded Age life for the Vanderbilt family across the harbor in Manhattan. (Courtesy of the Staten Island Museum at Snug Harbor.)

Shown is the Hudson River Railroad's freight depot at St. John's Park in 1868. Originally surrounded with fashionable townhouses, the park was owned by Trinity Church, an early Episcopal house of worship. Cornelius Vanderbilt purchased the parkland to construct the depot; eventually, the townhouses and church would be razed. (Courtesy of the Robert N. Dennis Collection in the NYPL Miriam and Ira D. Wallach Division of Art, Prints, and Photographs.)

Another view of the freight depot reveals a 12-foot bronze likeness of Cornelius Vanderbilt, designed by Albert de Groot (1810?–1884) and sculpted by Ernst Plassmann (1823–1873). Surrounding the statue is a large bronze frieze with imagery of his shipping and railroad empire. The monumental sum paid for the completion of the statue in 1869 was $500,000. The depot was razed in 1927, and the site is now a park at the Holland Tunnel's exit. (Courtesy of the Robert N. Dennis Collection in the NYPL Miriam and Ira D. Wallach Division of Art, Prints, and Photographs.)

This late-19th-century view shows an elevated railroad bridge at Harlem Flats on Fourth Avenue (now Park Avenue) between East 100th and 116th Streets in New York County. The wooden trestle span was constructed for temporary use during Fourth Avenue's railroad improvement plan. (Courtesy of the Robert N. Dennis Collection in the NYPL Miriam and Ira D. Wallach Division of Art, Prints, and Photographs.)

A closer view of the trestle bridge at Harlem Flats reveals the natural landscape of upper Manhattan before radical development and increased habitation. These 19th-century scenes would change after Cornelius Vanderbilt's expansion in Midtown. (Courtesy of the Robert N. Dennis Collection in the NYPL Miriam and Ira D. Wallach Division of Art, Prints, and Photographs.)

Photographed in 2016 is a seemingly inconsequential wall of stones in the private West End Towers Park. These stones once formed a massive embankment that allowed the Hudson River Railroad to traverse the natural terrain of Manhattan Island and passed through land now comprising the same park on West End Avenue between West Sixty-Third and Sixty-Fourth Streets. The topography was shaped with bays, inlets, and tidal lagoons, thus requiring elevated track. (Photograph by Gregory Bilotto.)

These are more stones from the Hudson River Railroad's 1847 embankment, constructed by the brilliant civil engineer John Bloomfield Jervis (1795–1885). The surviving stones in the 2016 photograph of the West End Towers Park were recovered from a 1994 archaeological excavation of the site during construction on the property. (Photograph by Gregory Bilotto.)

Pictured is the 19th-century Third Avenue Railroad Depot as published by E. & H.T. Anthony & Company. Edward (1819–1888) and Henry Tiebout (1814–1884) Anthony were brothers and owned a photography company located at 509 Broadway, opposite the Metropolitan Hotel in Manhattan. The depot supplied horse-drawn streetcars for passengers along the Third Avenue Railway System, which was later electrified in 1899. (Courtesy of the Robert N. Dennis Collection in the NYPL Miriam and Ira D. Wallach Division of Art, Prints, and Photographs.)

The next several E. & H.T. Anthony & Company stereoscopic views show the 1848-built High Bridge designed by John Bloomfield Jervis. The span was constructed as a section of the Croton Aqueduct System for transport of potable water to New York County. The view from the early 1850s is identified by the absence of pedestrian railings and railroad tracks, and with a construction hoist midspan. (Courtesy of the Robert N. Dennis Collection in the NYPL Miriam and Ira D. Wallach Division of Art, Prints, and Photographs.)

The High Bridge's location was considered to be hinterland and the span was itself regarded as a distant monument frequented for an occasional holiday, as seen in another stereoscopic view by the Anthony brothers. Consequently, numerous resort hotels built below the High Bridge on the Harlem River provided guests a countrified retreat by the 1870s. The view is datable to the same period. (Courtesy of the Robert N. Dennis Collection in the NYPL Miriam and Ira D. Wallach Division of Art, Prints, and Photographs.)

Benjamin West Kilburn (1827–1909) and brother Edward (1830–1884), both photographers from Littleton, New Hampshire, produced this early-1870s stereoscopic view of resort hotels at the High Bridge. The hotels identified are Aquatic and Woodbine. (Courtesy of the Robert N. Dennis Collection in the NYPL Miriam and Ira D. Wallach Division of Art, Prints, and Photographs.)

An 1870s view shows tracks from the NYCHRR. The railroad and development have reached the High Bridge. (Courtesy of the Robert N. Dennis Collection in the NYPL Miriam and Ira D. Wallach Division of Art, Prints, and Photographs.)

This E. & H.T. Anthony & Company stereoscopic view of the High Bridge from the early 1890s shows parkland created in the immediate area of the structure. The manicured parkland replaced resort hotel construction, as daily visitors were drawn to the waterfront. The High Bridge Water Tower is visible in the background; it was constructed from 1866 to 1872 by John Bloomfield Jervis to increase water pressure as the city's needs swelled. (Courtesy of the Robert N. Dennis Collection in the NYPL Miriam and Ira D. Wallach Division of Art, Prints, and Photographs.)

The next photographs from 2016 show the High Bridge and the immediate surrounding area. The hotels have long vanished, and the parkland has become overgrown. Replacing 19th-century development is the 20th-century Maj. William Francis Deegan Expressway, named after a military architect. During the expressway's construction from 1939 to 1956, the motorcar would surpass railroad travel. (Photograph by Gregory Bilotto.)

In 1927, five stone arches from the High Bridge portion spanning the Harlem River were removed. The magnificent stone arched bridge, once the sole source of city water, faced demolition in the 1920s, as water operations ended in 1917. Instead, a riveted-steel arch was added to allow passing ships an easier way of navigating the Harlem River. (Photograph by Gregory Bilotto.)

This view of the High Bridge, observed from Bronx County in 2016, is similar to the E. & H.T. Anthony and Company stereoscopic view taken nearly 180 years earlier. The bridge and waterfront were rendered inaccessible after the expressway's construction, eventually closing and fading in memories by the 1970s. Through grassroots support and local government, the High Bridge was restored and reopened for public use on June 9, 2015. (Photograph by Gregory Bilotto.)

A 2016 photograph with a view looking across the High Bridge span from Bronx County reveals the original walkway consisting of brickwork laid in a herringbone pattern. Below the decking is the pipeline, installed with a downward slope for transport of drinkable water. (Photograph by Gregory Bilotto.)

A 2016 image from the High Bridge walkway shows the changes since an 1870s view of the same area was recorded. The railroad's enlargement is evident with a substantial maintenance facility in the distance and a passing suburban train en route to Grand Central Terminal. The once far-off area has become built-up with numerous high-rise structures and the expressway. The terrain has been altered, the land graded, and all inshore bodies of water filled. (Photograph by Gregory Bilotto.)

The 1963-built Alexander Hamilton Bridge reveals a design similar to the steel-arched portion of the High Bridge spanning the Harlem River. The waterfront area below both bridges has recently been restored to parkland, making the High Bridge and waterfront once again accessible to visitors, as seen in this 2016 image. (Photograph by Gregory Bilotto.)

The next photographs from 2016 show abandoned stairs stretching across the hillside. Both authors had the opportunity to explore the hidden stairs, closed and overgrown, leading from the base of the High Bridge to its crossing. The entry and stairs were carved from large stones erected in the 19th century. (Photograph by Gregory Bilotto.)

Here is a north view of the remarkably preserved stairs. Along the climb, numerous derelict lampposts were observed. These match the existing lighting scheme across the span. The original Beaux-Arts design of the lampposts was done in cast iron between 1910 and 1912 by the architect Henry Bacon (1866–1924)—although those on both the stairs and bridge are likely steel and aluminium reproductions. Bacon worked for the firm McKim, Mead & White and his Beaux-Arts lampposts—called the Boulevard type—have been used over the last 100 years. (Photograph by Gregory Bilotto.)

Here is a view of the stairs looking down the hillside and eastward. The importance of the High Bridge has faded, both for the transport of water and as a symbolic barrier. It was formerly the 19th-century marker between farmland and hinterland at the fringe of Manhattan, and its symbolism was changed after Cornelius Vanderbilt's railroad brought development. (Photograph by Gregory Bilotto.)

An interior view from the 1880s shows the Vanderbilt family mausoleum under construction at the Moravian Cemetery in New Dorp, Richmond County. Designed by a proponent of the Beaux-Arts style, Richard Morris Hunt, it was uncharacteristically completed in the Romanesque Revival style from 1885 to 1886. The stone facade's three portals had cast-iron gates with the central portal featuring Christ enthroned. (Courtesy of the Miscellaneous Photo Collection in the LOC Prints and Photographs Division.)

Published under W.J. Grimshaw, this real-photo postcard, datable to the late 1880s–1890s, shows the finished Vanderbilt family mausoleum. The tomb and existing Moravian Cemetery grounds were built on land from the Vanderbilt estate. The cemetery was landscaped by the famous designer of Central Park, Frederick Law Olmsted (1822–1903). (Courtesy of the Staten Island Postcards Collection in the NYPL Irma and Paul Milstein Division of United States History, Local History, and Genealogy).

The Vanderbilt mausoleum as it exists today is shown in this 2016 photograph. It seems the Vanderbilt sepulchre and those interred within, including the commodore, cannot escape the ravages of time and judgement of history. The powerful monopoly has disappeared, and the lackluster monument, a product of the Gilded Age now absent gilding, is reminiscent of Roman Empire ruins. It represents faded glory and prosperity as the empire had fallen, and only blocks of stone remain witness. (Photograph by Gregory Bilotto.)

Two

GRAND, GRAND, GRAND! THE DEPOT AND STATION

The NYCHRR required a large structure in the 1860s for train housing, maintenance, and the facilitation of passenger transport, with enough area for expansion and to showcase its immense wealth and power. Cornelius Vanderbilt elected to buy numerous properties consisting of bogs, farms, and forested areas together with the immediate vicinity of Forty-Second Street, at the time occupied with tenement slums, industries, and railyard works. This unsuitable living environment and farmland would eventually total 47 acres in the area known today as Midtown Manhattan. The structure built was named Grand Central Depot, although at the time of construction, the notion that the depot was centralized led to mocking comments. The perception of most was that the area of the depot was basically uninhabitable and too far from the real city.

Nevertheless, Vanderbilt persevered in his vision to build an impressive depot, opening in 1871. Designed by the notable cast-iron architect John Butler Snook (1815–1901), the depot consolidated all rail travel departing and arriving in New York County from the three rail lines united under the NYCHRR. Steam-powered trains were prohibited below Forty-Second Street under an 1857 safety law, requiring the transfer of passengers to horse-drawn streetcars for completion of journeys. This law guided the selection process for the purchase of land and subsequent construction of the depot to the area of Forty-Second Street, as it was the furthest point mechanized trains could operate. The other structure built was a European-styled train shed, designed by the engineer Robert Griffith Hatfield (1815–1879). The metal fabrication was inspired by contemporary British examples and London's Crystal Palace. Assembled from wrought-iron Howe trusses, named after inventor William Howe (1803–1852), a 530-foot high vault was erected.

Upon completion of Grand Central Depot, development of the area that would become Midtown Manhattan was assured, as can be seen through the progression of numerous stereoscopic views of the zone. The transformation began with churches, housing, and other buildings erected along wide tree-lined avenues, similar to the boulevards of Paris. Within 15 years, however, it became apparent that the imposing depot could not manage the increasing volume and a new larger structure was intended for its replacement. Opening in 1900 and aptly named Grand Central Station, it would expand railroad travel and connect with the Interborough Rapid Transit (IRT) Third Avenue Line.

The next four views reveal the development around Grand Central Depot from the early 1870s to late 1880s. In this E. & H.T. Anthony & Company stereoscopic view, likely published near the depot's completion, excavation debris can be seen in the foreground, while in the background, the absence of large buildings should be noted. (Courtesy of the Robert N. Dennis Collection in the NYPL Miriam and Ira D. Wallach Division of Art, Prints, and Photographs.)

Grand Central Depot, with active construction in the foreground, bears the names NYCHRR, New York & Harlem River Railroad (NYHRR), and New York & New Haven Railroad (NYNHR). These three railroads all converged at the depot and were united under the control of Cornelius Vanderbilt. The original name for the depot would actually be Grand Union Depot. (Courtesy of the Robert N. Dennis Collection in the NYPL Miriam and Ira D. Wallach Division of Art, Prints, and Photographs.)

The depot had horse-drawn streetcars for conveyance of passengers. Note its large train shed. The view can be dated to 1871 as the NYNHR is displayed on the depot's exterior. In 1872, the same railroad line merged, becoming the New York, New Haven & Hartford Railroad (NYNHHR), and the name was changed. (Courtesy of the Robert N. Dennis Collection in the NYPL Miriam and Ira D. Wallach Division of Art, Prints, and Photographs.)

Grand Central Depot was styled after the impressive monuments and buildings of the French Second Empire style. More specifically, John Butler Snook looked to the designs of Parisian edifices built during the reign of Emperor Charles-Louis-Napoléon Bonaparte, also known as Napoléon III, (1808–1873). These are immediately recognizable in the view from the early 1870s. (Courtesy of the Robert N. Dennis Collection in the NYPL Miriam and Ira D. Wallach Division of Art, Prints, and Photographs.)

The zone around Grand Central Depot would become built-up, as shown in the view datable to the 1880s. Large buildings were situated along the tree-lined avenues. No structures, however, surpass the height of the depot. Construction debris can still be seen in the foreground. (Courtesy of the Robert N. Dennis Collection in the NYPL Miriam and Ira D. Wallach Division of Art, Prints, and Photographs.)

An interior stereoscopic view by E. & H.T. Anthony & Company shows the glass facade of Grand Central Depot's train shed. Through examination of Robert Griffith Hatfield's wrought-iron assembly, ornate decorative elements that adorn the Howe trusses and balustrades are noticeable, such as braided designs. The lampposts visible in the 1870s view were gas-lit, providing an ethereal glow at night. (Courtesy of the Robert N. Dennis Collection in the NYPL Miriam and Ira D. Wallach Division of Art, Prints, and Photographs.)

Another 1870s view shows the massive train shed's interior. The 90-foot-high wrought-iron and glass ceiling was permeated with natural light during the day, while 12 chandeliers provided illumination by night. The Howe trusses were painted in brilliant colors, and the lower sections were gilt. Emblazoned on the ceiling six feet high were the names of Cornelius Vanderbilt as the president and William Henry Vanderbilt (1821–1885) as the treasurer. (Courtesy of the Robert N. Dennis Collection in the NYPL Miriam and Ira D. Wallach Division of Art, Prints, and Photographs.)

Trains crowd the interior of Grand Central Depot's monumental carriage shed, almost the largest in the world at the time, in a view likely from the 1880s. The need, however, for a larger station and a solution to the overcrowded railyard would become more real. (Courtesy of the Robert N. Dennis Collection in the NYPL Miriam and Ira D. Wallach Division of Art, Prints, and Photographs.)

The Grand Union Hotel, built in 1868 and enlarged through successful years of business, is shown in this image from between 1910 and 1914. Originally constructed on land opposite the future Grand Central Depot, it would become the largest hotel in the city of New York. The hotel, high-rise buildings, and IRT Third Avenue Line, at left, demonstrate the creation of Midtown Manhattan. This photograph was made from a glass negative by the Detroit Publishing Company. (Courtesy of the Detroit Publishing Company Collection in the LOC Prints and Photographs Division.)

An advertisement shows the Grand Union Hotel, owned and operated under Simeon Ford and family until it was closed in 1914. The exaggerated Second Empire architecture of the hotel as shown in an 1893 publication falsely shows a third mansard pavilion. Many famous guests stayed the night, some ending in tragedy, such as Congressman Charles Addison Chickering (b. 1843), suspiciously falling to his death (possibly a murder) in 1900. The hotel was razed in 1914. (Courtesy of the Press Club Fair Official Programme in the NYPL Irma and Paul Milstein Division of United States History, Local History, and Genealogy).

Jouvin Hippolyte (1825–1889) produced this stereoscopic aerial view of the rue de Rivoli and the Grand Hôtel du Louvre, likely in the 1860s. These are examples of the Parisian building program in the Second Empire style. Highlights include mansard rooflines and pavilions set on wide boulevards, which influenced the design of Grand Central Depot. (Courtesy of the Stereograph Cards Collection in the LOC Prints and Photographs Division.)

A 1900 real-photo postcard shows the rue de Rivoli adjacent to the Palais des Tuileries in Paris. These grand tree-lined boulevards and buildings in the Second Empire style follow the urban planning of Baron Georges-Eugène Haussmann (1809–1891). Paris in the 1870s was radically reshaped, coinciding with the construction of Grand Central Depot. (Courtesy of the Photochrom Prints Collection in the LOC Prints and Photographs Division.)

The Palais des Tuileries was initially constructed in 1564 and underwent several renovations over the centuries, including the period of time during which the Second Empire style was popularized. The photographer Edouard Baldus (1813–1889) took this image, likely in the 1860s, revealing imperial influences characterized by mansard rooflines and pavilions. (Courtesy of the Miscellaneous Photo Collection in the LOC Prints and Photographs Division.)

The Palais du Louvre, built in 1546 and once a royal residence, is now home to the Musée du Louvre as shown in the 2011 image. The palace was redesigned in the 19th century to connect with the Palais des Tuileries as part of the Parisian building program. The mansard details of both palaces would have a direct impact on the design of Grand Central Depot. The Paris Commune burned and razed the Palais des Tuileries in 1871. (Photograph by Joaquim Alves Gaspar, courtesy of the Joaquim Alves Gaspar Collection).

This 2014 interior view shows the cast-iron train shed from the Gare du Nord, or North Station, in Paris, built from 1861 to 1864. The design and ornate details on the metalwork are similar to those of the shed constructed for Grand Central Depot. The 1868-built train shed from London's St. Pancras Railway Station would also influence the depot's shed design. The British example had a Gothic pointed arch supported with 688 cast-iron columns, while the depot's shed would utilize a segmented arch. (Photograph by David Iliff, courtesy of the David Iliff Collection).

The 1860-built London Victoria Station with its Second Empire–style facade is shown in a 2009 image. This French style with its imperial mansard design would have a resounding impact on period architecture in the United Kingdom and United States as numerous Anglo and American architects elected to study architecture in the École nationale supérieure des beaux-arts in Paris. (Photograph by Ewan Munro, courtesy of the Ewan Munro Collection).

As the son of William Kissam Vanderbilt and Alva Vanderbilt Belmont (1853–1933), William Kissam Vanderbilt II (1878–1944), pictured in 1903, spent his youth amid the ostentatious and wasteful nature characteristic of the Gilded Age. This was manifested in the homes in which he once resided, architecturally significant but overtly extravagant and excessive. Later, he became president of the NYCHRR and would live a lavish lifestyle of motorcar racing, traveling, and yachting. (Courtesy of the Miscellaneous Photo Collection in the LOC Prints and Photographs Division.)

An 1897 photograph by Benjamin J. Falk (1853–1925) shows the William Kissam Vanderbilt mansion built in the Châteauesque style. A combination of elements from both the French Renaissance and Gothic styles, it was constructed by Richard Morris Hunt from 1878 to 1882. An 1883 ball held for 1,000 guests in celebration of the opening by Alva Vanderbilt Belmont cost $3,000,000. The house was razed in 1926. (Courtesy of the Miscellaneous Photo Collection in the LOC Prints and Photographs Division.)

A second view shows the William Kissam Vanderbilt mansion at 660 Fifth Avenue between West Fifty-Second and Fifty-Third Streets in Manhattan. In this 1903 view looking north are the Episcopal St. Thomas Church built between 1865 and 1870 and Fifth Avenue Presbyterian Church of 1875. Burned in 1905, St. Thomas Church was rebuilt in the French High Gothic style from 1911 to 1913. (Courtesy of the Stereograph Cards Collection in the LOC Prints and Photographs Division.)

The 1901 photograph, made from a glass negative by the Detroit Publishing Company, depicts the residence of Cornelius Vanderbilt II, constructed in 1883 by noted architects George Browne Post (1837–1913) and Richard Morris Hunt and designed in the Châteauesque style. The interior was decorated by the French firm of Jules Allard et Fils. In this view looking south on Fifth Avenue, spires from the twin churches and the William Kissam Vanderbilt home are visible. (Courtesy of the Detroit Publishing Company Collection in the LOC Prints and Photographs Division.)

Upon completion, the home for Cornelius Vanderbilt II at 1 West Fifty-Seventh Street and Fifth Avenue became the largest private residence constructed in the city of New York, a title still held. The home was razed in the late 1920s and replaced with the Bergdorf Goodman department store. In this view looking north on Fifth Avenue, the upper floors of the 1907-built Plaza Hotel are visible. (Courtesy of the Detroit Publishing Company Collection in the LOC Prints and Photographs Division.)

The famous American photographer Irving Underhill (1872–1960) captured this view of the Cornelius Vanderbilt II home in 1921. The shift from residential and commercial on lower Fifth Avenue is noticeable with high-rise building construction, quite a contrast from 20 years earlier. Included among these high-rise structures is the 1921-built Heckscher Building (now Crown Building) by Warren & Wetmore. (Courtesy of the Miscellaneous Photo Collection in the LOC Prints and Photographs Division.)

This c. 1901 view shows the Bowery Savings Bank, located at 130 Bowery. Designed by the architect Stanford White (1853–1906) from the firm McKim, Mead & White, it was constructed from 1893 to 1895. The IRT Third Avenue Line ran elevated steam-powered carriages through the Bowery and along Third Avenue to reach the IRT platform at Grand Central Station. The name Bowery is derived from a Dutch word meaning farm. (Courtesy of the Detroit Publishing Company Collection in the LOC Prints and Photographs Division.)

Puffs of steam and loud noise accompany a steam-powered locomotive approaching the Bowery Savings Bank, built from 1896 to 1900. The elevated tracks were completed in 1878 and although safer than at-grade travel involving horse-drawn carriages, motorcars, and pedestrians, the elevated steam-powered locomotives remained dangerous, raucous, and aesthetically unpleasing, while continuing to pollute. (Courtesy of the Miscellaneous Photo Collection in the LOC Prints and Photographs Division.)

This 1900 view shows a steam-powered train at the platform on Bowery and Grand Streets. The New York Elevated Railway Company constructed the IRT Third Avenue Line from Battery Park to the Harlem River, quite an achievement since it was not uncommon during this period for numerous railway lines to open and fail throughout the city of New York. This was due to heavy competition and the unpopularity of the respective line. (Courtesy of the Detroit Publishing Company Collection in the LOC Prints and Photographs Division.)

A later scene with the Bowery Savings Bank from 1905 shows the dual elevated tracks of the IRT Third Avenue Line. Obscuring the bank's incredible Beaux-Arts facade is the south track. Although in place before the bank's construction, Stanford White must have shunned the elevated structure. The architect was murdered on June 25, 1906, but was consoled beforehand when, in 1902, the line was electrified, thus mitigating noise and pollution issues. (Courtesy of the Detroit Publishing Company Collection in the LOC Prints and Photographs Division.)

William Henry Jackson (1843–1942) captured this view of Grand Central Station in 1900, the year it opened. The new station was enlarged and redesigned, departing from the antiquated Second Empire style popularized by Cornelius Vanderbilt and his architects. The earlier wrought-iron train shed was retained, along with its problematic railyard. (Courtesy of the Detroit Publishing Company Collection in the LOC Prints and Photographs Division.)

This 1900–1903 view of Grand Central Station is looking down East Forty-Second Street. The station was designed in a Classical Revival style with temple elements by the architect Bradford Lee Gilbert (1853–1911). The interior offered a new grand waiting room designed by Samuel Huckel Jr. (1858–1917). It was a replacement for and improvement on three separate waiting rooms for the three rail lines of the depot. (Courtesy of the Detroit Publishing Company Collection in the LOC Prints and Photographs Division.)

A 1904–1906 view down East Forty-Second Street shows Grand Central Station with numerous cast-iron eagles adorning its facade. Farther down are Madison Avenue and, opening in 1896, the Manhattan Hotel, designed by the famous hotel architect Henry Janeway Hardenbergh (1847–1918). Even farther is the 1904-built New York Times Building in the square carrying the newspaper company's name. (Courtesy of the Detroit Publishing Company Collection in the LOC Prints and Photographs Division.)

A September 8, 1908, view of the East Forty-Second Street entrance to Grand Central Station shows hurrying passengers. Newly electrified streetcars and horse-drawn carriages fill the background, transferring those arriving and departing the station for travel in Lower Manhattan. New improvements, including elevators, steam heat, a modern powerhouse, and electric lighting, would facilitate easier travel through the station. (Courtesy of the Bain News Service Collection in the LOC Prints and Photographs Division.)

The photographer described this view looking down Vanderbilt Avenue from East Forty-Second Street dated September 8, 1908, as a returning summer crowd. The cast-iron and arc-shaped lamppost in the far left is classified as a Bishop Crook type with a garland. The arc-shaped lamppost from the previous image is a wrought iron Bishop Crook-type variation with a garland. Both lampposts show the results of electrification; unfortunately, few remain today. (Courtesy of the Bain News Service Collection in the LOC Prints and Photographs Division.)

To the far right in this 1904–1906 view of Grand Central Station from East Forty-Second Street are the annex and IRT Third Avenue Line elevated station. The 1885-built annex provided additional tracks and platforms to accommodate increased passenger use at the depot. A diminutive version of the depot, it was designed in the Second Empire style and survived the depot's transformation to a station. (Courtesy of the Bain News Service Collection in the LOC Prints and Photographs Division.)

Seated passengers await departure in the elegant waiting room of Grand Central Station in a 1904 image. The refined interior by Samuel Huckel Jr. features hardwood benches, globe-shaped lamps, ornate walls, and a high ceiling with a border noting the name of each major station on the NYCHRR line. (Courtesy of the Detroit Publishing Company Collection in the LOC Prints and Photographs Division.)

On Christmas Day 1908, a crowd carrying baskets waits with eagerness for entry to a dinner hosted by the Salvation Army at Grand Central Palace. Grand Central Palace, built in 1893 and located on Lexington Avenue between East Forty-Third and Forty-Fourth Streets, served as an exhibition hall. It was razed in 1913 for construction of Grand Central Terminal. (Courtesy of the Bain News Service Collection in the LOC Prints and Photographs Division.)

The next three 2016 photographs show a selection of the cast-iron eagles that would survive the demolition of Grand Central Station. The eagles, with a wingspan stretching 14 feet, were once proudly perched high atop the station but have been relocated several times since their initial removal. This eagle, coated in black, is one of a pair from the estate of William Kissam Vanderbilt II in Centerport, New York, on Long Island. The estate was aptly named Eagle's Nest. (Photograph by Gregory Bilotto.)

Both authors had the pleasure to search for a select group of the remaining eagles from Grand Central Station, and together located a pair in Garrison, New York. The two eagles were situated on a rock outcropping overlooking the drive of the St. Basil Academy of the Greek Orthodox Archdiocese in America. The school property was a former country estate ironically named Eagle's Rest. (Photograph by Gregory Bilotto.)

A view of the cobbled drive shows the gatehouse of the William Kissam Vanderbilt II country estate. The Mediterranean-influenced Eagle's Nest was designed in the Spanish Colonial Revival style by the firm Warren & Wetmore from 1910 to 1936. The architects, partners in the design of Grand Central Terminal, departed from French elegance to erect the 24-room house according to the Vanderbilt family's wishes. (Photograph by Gregory Bilotto.)

Known as Marble House, the Gilded Age mansion in this 2014 image was a home of William Kissam Vanderbilt and wife, Alva Vanderbilt Belmont. It stands at 596 Bellevue Avenue in Newport, Rhode Island, and was built between 1888 and 1892 by Richard Morris Hunt. The residence, designed to reflect elements from both the Petit Trianon at the Château de Versailles and the White House, cost $11,000,000. The lion's share was spent on marble. The extravagance of the period is reflected in the architecture, especially since the Vanderbilts classified it a mere cottage, owing to its use only a few weeks during the summer. (Photograph by Gregory Bilotto.)

Three

BUILDING GRAND CENTRAL TERMINAL AND OPENING DAY

An architectural competition was organized in 1903, and four submissions in the Beaux-Arts style were received from prominent American architectural firms, inspired by the numerous avant-garde architectural styles at the 1893 World's Columbian Exposition in Chicago. The lead architects, all with varied visions for the future terminal, included Samuel Huckel Jr., Daniel Burnham (1846–1912), Stanford White, and Charles A. Reed (1858–1911) with Allen H. Stem (1856–1931). The architectural firm of Reed & Stem, notable for numerous railroad projects, was selected for the new terminal and surrounding structures, becoming the terminal zone. Charles A. Reed was also the brother-in-law of William John Wilgus. The unsuccessful architects, however, would apply their terminal designs to other projects, and nearly all would be constructed reflecting their original plans. Stanford White's architectural firm of McKim, Mead & White would apply its design, titled the Court of Honor, which included a tower that would have been the world's tallest building, to the Municipal Building for the City of New York. Daniel Burnham would see his Beaux-Arts terminal design realized through the construction of Union Station in Washington, DC.

William Kissam Vanderbilt however became exceedingly uneasy after the completion of Pennsylvania Station by Stanford White and his architectural firm. Thereafter, he elected to hire the architectural firm Warren & Wetmore, thus forming the Associated Architects partnership with Reed & Stem. Whitney Warren (1864–1943), a Vanderbilt cousin, was trained in the French style at the Parisian École nationale supérieure des beaux-arts, as were nearly all of the those involved with the terminal project. Warren's rival French design, influenced by medieval cathedrals and classical Roman triumphal arches, dominated the Reed & Stem vision. After the death of Charles Reed in 1911, Warren and Charles Delevan Wetmore (1866–1941) assumed control of the terminal project and sidestepped the Reed & Stem firm. A lawsuit soon followed, which was resolved in 1922, with the court finding in favor of Reed & Stem. An award was ordered for $500,000 in damages, and Warren was expelled from the American Institute of Architects for unprofessional conduct. The creation of the unique terminal and its surrounding area would not have been possible, however, without the collaboration of both firms. Reed & Stem provided the practical railroading design; Warren & Wetmore, the classical- and French-styled decoration. Perhaps, Warren's ultimate tribute to the Vanderbilts, expressed throughout the terminal decorative program, was the overt application of the Vanderbilt acorn and oak leaves. Alva Vanderbilt Belmont had created the blazon, after inspiration from a poem penned by David Everett (1769–1813) that contains a line about tall oak trees grown from tiny acorns. This indicated the Vanderbilt family, although with humble origins, had risen to great prominence.

In one of perhaps the only existing images of Park Avenue's railroad tunnel collision, the rear carriage of train No. 223 carrying New Rochelle passengers is shown in the aftermath on January 8, 1902. The force of the impact is evident; however, most actually perished in the escaping steam from the locomotive pulling the White Plains suburban train. This photograph was taken by a NYCHRR photographer. (Courtesy of the New York Railroad Enthusiasts' Arthur Bateman Corthell Collection in the Frederick Ely Williamson Library at Grand Central Terminal.)

The crash occurred below the East Fifty-Sixth Street vent, which was insufficient in alleviating poor visibility. A diaphanous glow illuminates support piers, as spectators viewing from above are shielded from falling snow with an open umbrella. The motorman John Martin Wisker had resided at 314 East 157th Street in Bronx County, near the Park Avenue tracks. Unjustly tried for manslaughter, but later acquitted, he was haunted by the tragedy and drowned (possibly a suicide) on August 11, 1909. This photograph (the other extant image of the incident) was taken by a NYCHRR photographer. (Courtesy of the New York Railroad Enthusiasts' Arthur Bateman Corthell Collection in the Frederick Ely Williamson Library at Grand Central Terminal.)

Park Avenue's railroad tunnel entrance begins at East Ninety-Seventh Street in Manhattan, which is shown in the 2016 photograph. Trains had operated in the below-grade tunnel to improve conditions since the late 19th century, with a series of vents utilized before electrification allowing smoke and steam an exit. After electrification, the vents were masked in the avenue's planted central divider, completing the transition from Fourth Avenue to Park Avenue. (Photograph by Gregory Bilotto.)

William John Wilgus is pictured in the early 1900s, and at the time was chief civil engineer for the NYCHRR. The genius behind railroad modernization, electrification, the terminal's construction, and the air rights concept would resign following the February 16, 1907, derailment of an electrified train at Woodlawn in Bronx County. The railroad line through Woodlawn, where 20 died, had been electrified the previous day. This photograph was taken by a NYCHRR photographer. (Courtesy of the Arthur Bateman Corthell Collection in the New York Railroad Enthusiast Archives of the Frederick Ely Williamson Library at Grand Central Terminal.)

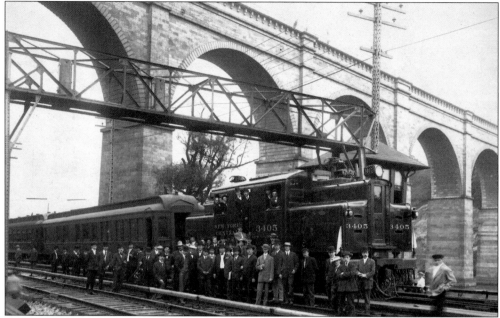

On September 30, 1906, the electrified train trial commences from the High Bridge base to Grand Central Station, an international event attracting engineers, motormen, and the press to witness the first of its kind in North America. The S-Motor No. 3405, built by the American Locomotive and General Electric Companies in 1901, leads the train to Midtown. This photograph was taken by a NYCHRR photographer. (Courtesy of the William John Wilgus Papers in the NYPL Irma and Paul Milstein Division of United States History, Local History, and Genealogy).

A second NYCHRR photograph taken at the High Bridge shows S-Motor No. 3406 on electrified track. Crowds have gathered to view the new locomotive and carriages, while a photographer has paused with equipment in the foreground. The S-Motors were developed and originally tested in Schenectady, New York. (Courtesy of the William John Wilgus Papers in the NYPL Irma and Paul Milstein Division of United States History, Local History, and Genealogy).

A third NYCHRR photograph shows S-Motor No. 3405 at Grand Central Station, having successfully completed the trial. Crowds have gathered at Vanderbilt's train shed and peer over the elevated walkway. (Courtesy of the William John Wilgus Papers in the NYPL Irma and Paul Milstein Division of United States History, Local History, and Genealogy).

Dated July 26, 1906, this is a closer view of the S-Motor locomotive No. 3401. Photographed at Kingsbridge in Bronx County by a NYCHRR photographer, the electric engine could advance or reverse without use of a turntable and dramatically reduced railroad injuries and deaths, despite the Woodlawn derailment. (Courtesy of the William John Wilgus Papers in the NYPL Irma and Paul Milstein Division of United States History, Local History, and Genealogy).

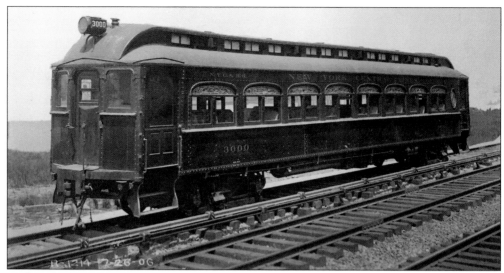

A closer look at a Steel Suburban Car, motor No. 3000—also photographed at Kingsbridge by a NYCHRR photographer—reveals riveted-steel construction, which was engineered to be non-collapsible and fireproof. These motors were utilized for short-distance suburban trips. (Courtesy of the William John Wilgus Papers in the NYPL Irma and Paul Milstein Division of United States History, Local History, and Genealogy).

Dated July 27, 1906, an interior view of a Steel Suburban Car—perhaps the same viewed at Kingsbridge—shows luxurious furnishings. Wide seats and aisles, dual baggage racks, shaded windows, and electric lighting provided great comfort for passengers. This image was taken by a NYCHRR photographer. (Courtesy of the William John Wilgus Papers in the NYPL Irma and Paul Milstein Division of United States History, Local History, and Genealogy).

This November 19, 1906, NYCHRR panoramic view of Grand Central Station displays the chaos before the electrification process was fully operational. The first electric trial, realized less than two months earlier, led to replacement of the dangerous and polluting steam locomotives with electric engines. On the right-hand side of the photograph, one can see carriages crowding the railyard, and a closer look reveals the newly electrified third rails. Construction for the new terminal had already commenced at East Fiftieth Street, north of this scene. The Belmont (center) and Manhattan (right of center) Hotels are visible in the distance. (Courtesy of the William John Wilgus Papers in the NYPL Irma and Paul Milstein Division of United States History, Local History, and Genealogy).

The Belmont Hotel by Warren & Wetmore, in the Beaux-Arts style with Edwardian influences, was completed for August Belmont Jr. (1858–1924) of the Belmont Hotel Company in 1904–1908. The hotel, the tallest in the world upon completion, was famous for suicides. One incident involved a doctor's 28-year old butler, Jergen E. Muhlensteth (b. 1881), who jumped to his death through the glass-ceilinged lobby. It was razed in 1931. The 1908–1909 image also shows a cast-iron eagle atop Grand Central Station on the right. (Courtesy of the Detroit Publishing Company Collection in the LOC Prints and Photographs Division.)

The 1896 Manhattan Hotel, designed by the famous hotel architect Henry Janeway Hardenbergh, is shown in an early-1900s image. The architect had designed the Waldorf, Astoria, and Plaza hotels; the Waldorf and Astoria merged in 1897. Built in the French (upper section) and Italian Renaissance (lower section) styles with interiors by Louis Comfort Tiffany, it was replaced with a 40-story high-rise in 1964. (Courtesy of the Detroit Publishing Company Collection in the LOC Prints and Photographs Division.)

THE F. & M. Schaefer Brewing

R-1588-8-31-06

C.C. YARD IMP EXCAVATION BETWEEN 49-50 ST

A trench is excavated between East Forty-Ninth and Fifty-First Streets on August 31, 1906. In this view looking north, a Madison Avenue pedestrian bridge spans the work and a building operated by the F. & M. Schaefer Brewing Company is on the right. The company, founded by brothers Frederick (1817–1897) and Maximilian Karl Emil (1819–1904) Schaefer, maintained a vast brewery at the Park Avenue site, which was sold later as real estate values soared. This photograph was taken by a NYCHRR photographer. (Courtesy of the William John Wilgus Papers in the NYPL Irma and Paul Milstein Division of United States History, Local History, and Genealogy).

Taken by a NYCHRR photographer on September 12, 1906, this image shows construction through Fourth Avenue, or the future Park Avenue, with excavations for the new subterranean railyard. Pedestrian bridges connect Lexington Avenue on the right to Madison Avenue. The view north reveals progress on the massive substation, built as a part of the terminal's electrification process. (Courtesy of the William John Wilgus Papers in the NYPL Irma and Paul Milstein Division of United States History, Local History, and Genealogy).

In a view looking north toward the substation, excavation for the railyard continues in this 1908 image. The O'Rourke Engineering and Construction Company was responsible for the annual removal of 400 carloads of rock and earth, over 10 years, totalling 2,800,000 cubic yards. On the right, trains operate on tracks undisturbed. Excavation work was divided into sections, thus allowing the railroad to remain functional. (Courtesy of the Detroit Publishing Company Collection in the LOC Prints and Photographs Division.)

An image taken by a NYCHRR photographer on September 21, 1906, from East Fifty-First Street with a view looking toward Lexington Avenue shows the substation under construction. Workman maneuver steam-powered heavy equipment to set steel construction into place. (Courtesy of the Arthur Bateman Corthell Collection in the New York Railroad Enthusiast Archives of the Frederick Ely Williamson Library at Grand Central Terminal.)

This panorama, taken by a NYCHRR photographer and dated October 1, 1907, surveys the railyard from East Fiftieth Street in a view looking south and southwest. Grand Central Post Office is nearing completion, while the station and train shed flanked with the dual luxury hotels remain. Excavation of the yard continues. The right-hand side of the photograph shows that the electrification process has not been completed, as steam puffs from locomotives in the railyard are visible. Upon completion, 32 miles of electrified track would fill the terminal's complex, requiring the demolition of countless buildings. (Courtesy of the William John Wilgus Papers in the NYPL Irma and Paul Milstein Division of United States History, Local History, and Genealogy).

A new Grand Central Palace, completed in 1911 by the Associated Architects in the Beaux-Arts style, replaced the former, which was razed for terminal zone construction in 1913. The grand exhibition hall and high-rise office building opened on East Forty-Sixth Street between Lexington and Fourth Avenues. The May 2, 1911, image reveals work on the double-level railyard under the future Park Avenue, and the terminal's Beaux-Arts powerhouse is on the left. (Photograph by Irving Underhill, courtesy of the Miscellaneous Photo Collection in the LOC Prints and Photographs Division.)

The John Pierce Company, general contractor for the terminal project, required 18,000 tons of steel for the complex, which was then clad in stone masonry consisting of Connecticut granite and Indiana limestone. The roof was sheathed in copper. With a view looking south toward the Belmont Hotel, the 1910–1912 image shows the double-level subterranean railyard below the terminal and Vanderbilt Avenue. (Courtesy of the Detroit Publishing Company Collection in the LOC Prints and Photographs Division.)

The results of Grand Central Terminal's architectural competition were manifested in other railroad projects, as photographed in 2015. The Associated Architects partnership utilized a version of Reed & Stem's original terminal proposal, the Court of Honor, for the Michigan Central Station in Detroit. The grand station complex with an immense office tower above, completed in the Beaux-Arts style, opened in 1913. (Photograph by Gregory Bilotto.)

A closer view from 2015 of the derelict Detroit station reveal design and decorative elements with corollaries found in Grand Central Terminal. Architecturally connected to the terminal, it almost went under the wrecking ball in 2009 but was saved through grassroots action and historic preservation laws. (Photograph by Gregory Bilotto.)

Another unsuccessful entry from the architectural competition, proposed by McKim, Mead & White, was incorporated into the Municipal Building for the City of New York in 1914. The David N. Dinkins Municipal Building retains numerous sections from the firm's original design, particularly a clock tower. This element appears in this 2016 image as the building's apex, crowning the dramatic Beaux-Arts facade. (Photograph by Gregory Bilotto.)

Although officially opened in 1913, the terminal nears completion in this 1914–1915 image, and the Park Avenue Viaduct remains unfinished. Neither the viaduct's span over East Forty-Second Street, modeled after the Beaux-Arts bridge named for Tsar Alexander III (1845–1894) in Paris, nor Pershing Square has been built yet. The IRT Third Avenue station is visible on the right, and the terminal remains striking, without any high-rises obstructing its view. (Courtesy of the Bain News Service Collection in the LOC Prints and Photographs Division.)

This American Studio–produced 1920 view shows a section of the bridge, now complete, connecting the Park Avenue Viaduct with Park Avenue South. The terminal's elevated drive was revolutionary in design, permitting motorcars to easily traverse the vital avenue while allowing others below direct access. A fault of the Michigan Central Station was that it was designed with limited motorcar accessibility and thus declined more rapidly. (Courtesy of Miscellaneous Photo Collection in the LOC Prints and Photographs Division.)

A series of photographs was taken in February 1913, before the terminal opened to the public. The night sky from October to March with images of the zodiac constellations is painted on the ceiling in the main concourse. The French portraitist Paul-César Helleu (1859–1927) was asked by Whitney Warren to design the ceiling, incorporating 2,500 stars and 65 electric lightbulbs to outline the largest, done in blue and gold highlighting. Despite intense planning, the constellations were mistakenly painted in reverse and remains so to this day. (Courtesy of the Detroit Publishing Company Collection in the LOC Prints and Photographs Division.)

This is a view of the grand staircase, which exits to Vanderbilt Avenue. Whitney Warren relied on the stairs and interior of the Palais Garnier, the grand opera house of Paris, although inverted, in shaping the terminal's grand entry. The design of three large arched arcades above the Paris stairs has similarly been placed in the terminal (as fenestrations), including the pediment and balustrades. (Courtesy of the Detroit Publishing Company Collection in the LOC Prints and Photographs Division.)

The main waiting room, adorned in splendor with hardwood seating and tropical plants and situated below gilt chandeliers, provided a luxurious respite for passengers. In this image, natural lighting floods the room, illuminating ornate stone-carved French details. (Courtesy of the Detroit Publishing Company Collection in the LOC Prints and Photographs Division.)

A view shows the private ladies' sitting room, complete with comfortable furnishings and facilities for the lavatory and telephone. (Courtesy of the Detroit Publishing Company Collection in the LOC Prints and Photographs Division.)

At the bottom of this incline, one will find access to suburban trains and to the restaurant. The entire terminal complex was designed with numerous rises, expediting passenger travel throughout. Several studies were undertaken during planning involving women with children, passengers with luggage, and others in determining the most efficient form of mobility. (Courtesy of the Detroit Publishing Company Collection in the LOC Prints and Photographs Division.)

Pictured is the interior of the Oyster Bar, located at the base of the rise from the main concourse to the suburban level. Ornate Guastavino tiles, developed by Rafael Guastavino (1842–1908) from Valencia, Spain, cover the vaults of the restaurant. His tiling process combined structural integrity with beauty, using multilayered tiles, mortar and plaster for strength, and then decorative glaze to sheath the tiles. (Courtesy of the Detroit Publishing Company Collection in the LOC Prints and Photographs Division.)

Through the Guastavino Fireproof Construction Company, his tiling was utilized in the vaults below the main concourse and the base of each rise, as shown in the image. It was also employed in tunnels connecting luxury hotels with the terminal. Rafael Guastavino would later die in North Carolina after work on Biltmore House, the largest private residence in American history, belonging to George Washington Vanderbilt II (1862–1914). (Courtesy of the Detroit Publishing Company Collection in the LOC Prints and Photographs Division.)

In this view of the suburban-level concourse, a central rise flows from the main concourse above. Elaborate French details are visible throughout, outlining the floor and ceiling. (Courtesy of the Detroit Publishing Company Collection in the LOC Prints and Photographs Division.)

Rows of illuminated ticket windows line the suburban level's south side, while the north side provides access to track platforms. (Courtesy of the Detroit Publishing Company Collection in the LOC Prints and Photographs Division.)

Framing Grand Central Terminal in this 1920s American Studio photograph are the Belmont Hotel and 1884-built Murray Hill Hotel on the left, vestiges of Grand Central Station, while the c. 1922 Pershing Square Building is on the right. The Park Avenue Viaduct, interrupted by the IRT Third Avenue Line platform, remains incomplete. The 1919 copyright date is incorrect for obvious reasons. (Courtesy of Miscellaneous Photo Collection in the LOC Prints and Photographs Division.)

A trio of luxurious hotels was built around Grand Central Terminal to serve increased passenger volume. The hotels were all directly connected to the terminal facilitating easier access. The 1919-built, Beaux-Arts–style Commodore Hotel by Warren & Wetmore is shown adjacent to the terminal on East Forty-Second Street in an image of the same year. The vacant lot on the right, formerly the Grand Union Hotel site, will soon be home to the Pershing Square Building. (Photograph by Irving Underhill, courtesy of the Miscellaneous Photo Collection in the LOC Prints and Photographs Division.)

The 1924 Roosevelt Hotel is a second building of the trio and remains operational today, as viewed from East Forty-Fifth Street and Madison Avenue in this 2016 image. Named after Pres. Theodore Roosevelt (1858–1919) and built by the architect George Browne Post in the Beaux-Arts style, following Warren & Wetmore's vision. The interior lobby retains much of its original grandeur. (Photograph by Gregory Bilotto.)

A third building of the grand trio is the Biltmore Hotel, completed in 1913 by Warren & Wetmore and perhaps the most famous of the three hotels. In 1915, World War I peace negotiations, hosted by Henry Ford (1863–1947), took place at the Biltmore Hotel, and later, in 1916, the Treaty of the Danish West Indies (US Virgin Islands today) was signed transferring possession to America. The Roosevelt Hotel is on the right side in this 1920s Byron Company image. (Courtesy of the Pageant of America Collection in the NYPL Irma and Paul Milstein Division of United States History, Local History, and Genealogy).

Grand Central Post Office, built from 1906 to 1909 in the Beaux-Arts style, matched the construction and facade of the terminal. Trains originally connected with the post office for easy distribution of mail, a service replaced today with trucks. The building's air rights were utilized in 1992 with completion of the 38-story office tower at 450 Lexington Avenue, as captured in this 2015 photograph. (Photograph by Gregory Bilotto.)

In 1929, the crown of the terminal zone, completed in the Beaux-Arts style by Warren & Wetmore, was the New York Central Railroad (NYCR) Building. Towering above the terminal and Park Avenue in this 1930s image, it offered glamorous offices for the railroad's administration and other tenants, such as Prohibition-era organized-crime operations. Powerful mobsters needed offices befitting their status, and the tower provided the appropriate setting. Their offices were retrofitted with hidden rooms and staircases, recently uncovered during renovations. (Collection of Gregory Bilotto.)

The 1893 Waldorf-Astoria Hotel, built in the German Renaissance style by architect Henry Janeway Hardenbergh, is shown in a 1904 image with the Knickerbocker Trust Company Building. The hotel, located at East Thirty-Third Street and Fifth Avenue, was the realization of Viscount William Waldorf Astor (1848–1919), but was razed in 1929 for construction of the Empire State Building. (Courtesy of the Detroit Publishing Company Collection in the LOC Prints and Photographs Division.)

The new Waldorf-Astoria Hotel (right), built in 1931, replaced Warren & Wetmore's Beaux-Arts Grand Central Terminal powerhouse. The hotel and nearby General Electric Building, both in the Art Deco style, tower above St. Bartholomew's Episcopal Church in this 1936 image, as air rights became more valuable. (Photograph by Berenice Abbott, courtesy of the Changing New York Collection in the NYPL Irma and Paul Milstein Division of United States History, Local History, and Genealogy).

Included in the Associated Architects' early-1900s designs and plans, devised by William John Wilgus, are grand railroad stations for Bronx County. Although never built, these and other proposed stations were intended to alleviate congestion of merging railroad lines in the electrified zone. Reproduced from an NYCHRR artist's watercolor rendering is a station below the High Bridge. (Courtesy of the William John Wilgus Papers in the NYPL Irma and Paul Milstein Division of United States History, Local History, and Genealogy).

A second watercolor, likely for Mott Haven, Bronx County, reveals a grand station in the Beaux-Arts style. The NYCHRR artist's watercolor rendering shows details reminiscent of Grand Central Terminal and resembles an earlier plan intended for the terminal itself. (Courtesy of the William John Wilgus Papers in the NYPL Irma and Paul Milstein Division of United States History, Local History, and Genealogy).

The elegant Grand Central Terminal Restaurant, which included the Oyster Bar, operated under the Union News Company in Grand Central Terminal. The restaurant had three daily menus, always changing to provide passengers the latest specialities, as described in this day menu dated November 17, 1917. The pricing is in cents. (Courtesy of the Frank E. Buttolph Menu Collection in the NYPL Rare Book Division.)

A Grand Central Terminal Restaurant menu dated December 5, 1917, shows selections available for dinner, with a suggestion to visit the First World War exhibition *Hero Land* at Grand Central Palace. The exhibition was charged with raising funds, revealing scenes from the war, and generating support for American and Allied forces. The exhibition would run from November 24 to December 12, 1917, and admission was 50¢. (Courtesy of the Frank E. Buttolph Menu Collection in the NYPL Rare Book Division.)

The next several 1917 photographs show visitors to the exhibition along with Allied forces' military equipment (including a British tank), a captured German submarine, five motion picture theaters, an ice-skating rink, restaurants, and other entertainment. Additionally, in *Hero Land* were re-created battlefields, bomb shelters, forts, trenches, a grand ballroom from the Château de Versailles, and streets of Baghdad. A French field cannon is pictured here. (Courtesy of the Bain News Service Collection in the LOC Prints and Photographs Division.)

A pair of French field mortars, among other artillery equipment from the First World War, is pictured at the exhibition. (Courtesy of the Bain News Service Collection in the LOC Prints and Photographs Division.)

The Marquis Charles Jean Marie Melchior de Polignac (1880–1950) stands with a destroyed French ambulance. The French aristocrat came to America to promote participation in the war. In October, before the exhibition, he married Nina Floyd Crosby, the widow of US senator James Biddle Eustis. (Courtesy of the Bain News Service Collection in the LOC Prints and Photographs Division.)

Clementine Blessing, shown with French artillery, is dressed in the traditional clothing of the Alsace-Lorraine region in France. Numerous visitors to the exhibition posed for similar photographs. (Courtesy of the Bain News Service Collection in the LOC Prints and Photographs Division.)

Kathryn S. Butterfield, another visitor to the exhibition, poses with French artillery. (Courtesy of the Bain News Service Collection in the LOC Prints and Photographs Division.)

The photographer captured Mrs. Earl Rankin in a likely Allied airplane shown at the exhibition. (Courtesy of the Bain News Service Collection in the LOC Prints and Photographs Division.)

At the close of the First World War in 1918, an international flower show was held at Grand Central Palace and included was a picture gallery with painted imagery from the war. Mrs. Newbold Le Roy Edgar stands with paintings depicting the conflict in Serbia. (Courtesy of the Bain News Service Collection in the LOC Prints and Photographs Division.)

At the same picture gallery, a photograph of Lt. Joseph Charles Stehlin (1897–1967), an American pilot, was taken. The lieutenant wears a uniform from the French Air Forces' Lafayette Escadrille, which consisted of American pilots that joined the French air war. (Courtesy of the Bain News Service Collection in the LOC Prints and Photographs Division.)

After the war, construction of the terminal zone continued following the Associated Architects' principles, with architecture similar in height and design to the terminal itself. John Merven Carrère (1858–1911) and Thomas Hastings (1860–1929) formed the architectural firm Carrère & Hastings, which designed the Liggett Building. The 1921 photograph shows construction reaching 23 stories for drugstore chain Liggett Company. (Photograph by Irving Underhill, courtesy of the Miscellaneous Photo Collection in the LOC Prints and Photographs Division.)

The Postum Building was built in 1925 by the architectural firm Cross & Cross. Brothers John Walter (1878–1951) and Eliot (1884–1949) Cross were equally faithful to the terminal zone concept. Constructed in the Beaux-Arts and Classical Revival styles for the Postum Cereal Company (Post Cereals today), it is one of the few original buildings of the terminal zone still standing, as seen here in 2016. (Photograph by Gregory Bilotto.)

Four

BRANCH STATIONS AND POWER STRUCTURES

Grand Central Terminal's building program through the Associated Architects partnership included the design and construction of various suburban railroad stations. The new stations would facilitate easier travel on lines north of Grand Central Terminal and would provide baggage facilities, waiting rooms, and ticket offices. A variety of architectural designs and styles were employed for these structures, from simple brick facades expressing French influences to Tudor Revival, Mission Revival, Spanish Colonial Revival, and Beaux-Arts styles. French designs would, however, dominate and be blended with the avant-garde architectural styles presented at the World's Columbian Exposition in Chicago., such as Mission Revival and Beaux-Arts. The stations would also reflect interior and exterior architectural details from Grand Central Terminal, including the station furniture.

The railroad stations were constructed from 1909 to 1918 and involved the elimination of dangerous at-grade crossings between motorcars, pedestrians, and trains, creating instead underpasses or overpasses for motorcar and pedestrian use. The planning and layout was completed by Reed & Stem, and the architectural designs were largely finished by Warren & Wetmore. After the death of Charles A. Reed, credit for the suburban stations was disproportionately awarded to Warren & Wetmore. Additionally, Reed & Stem constructed numerous powerhouses, substations, and other support structures during the period of rail electrification, from 1903 to 1907. These structures generated electricity to power the trains from the subterranean railyard to the North White Plains and Croton-Harmon stations and illuminated Grand Central Terminal and its suburban stations.

Eleven of the surviving original railroad stations in New York State are arranged chronologically by construction date, with the powerhouses, substations, and support structures following respectively. Both authors had the pleasure to visit each structure original to Grand Central Terminal's building program, an enormous undertaking as the locations stretched from New York City through Westchester and Dutchess Counties into the Catskills, with one at the Canadian border. Moreover, several structures exist in a ruinous state, making the task of visiting complicated and access difficult. Certain railroad stations and power structures were unfortunately razed and rebuilt in a modern style and were thus omitted, no longer reflective of the building program. These include the rebuilt Beacon (1918), Ludlow (1909–1918), Ossining (1910), and White Plains (1915) stations and the demolished Watertown (1909–1918) railroad station, Port Morris powerhouse (1903–1906), and High Bridge signal tower (c. 1903–1907), among others.

This mid-1930s real-photo postcard shows the railroad station in Scarsdale. Printed with an undivided back by the Artvue Postcard Company, formerly of 225 Fifth Avenue in Manhattan; the company produced collotypes for use as postcards. A collotype is a high-quality monotone photograph produced from a sheet of light-sensitive gelatin exposed photographically to an image, with no screen utilized. (Collection of Gregory Bilotto.)

The next several 2015 photographs show the NYCHRR railroad station for Scarsdale. Built in 1904 by the architect Grant Nichols, it was subsequently redesigned between 1909 and 1918 by the Associated Architects to match other suburban stations on the line. The station was completed in the Tudor Revival style, with exposed timber and stucco. The roof was covered with beautiful aquamarine and green terra-cotta tiles in the Spanish Colonial Revival style. (Photograph by Gregory Bilotto.)

An interior view of the railroad station shows hardwood seating and Guastavino tiling. The design and shape of the hardwood benches with rounded seating and ends was commonly seen at the suburban stations from Grand Central Terminal. Unique to Scarsdale, however, were the wrought-iron armrests, perhaps an early innovation or later addition. A fireplace was built in the waiting room. (Photograph by Gregory Bilotto.)

The magnificent tiling continues from the station house to the covered stairs and pedestrian bridge that spans the tracks. Scarsdale remains—or was the only—suburban station with this distinctive terra-cotta tiled color scheme in the Spanish Colonial Revival style. (Photograph by Gregory Bilotto.)

The pedestrian bridge was constructed of riveted steel and was painted dark green. Glass-paned windows were installed along the length of the stairs and bridge, providing natural lighting in the day hours. Lamps provided illumination at night. The pedestrian bridge and stairs were from a typical design repeated at nearly all suburban stations completed by the Associated Architects. (Photograph by Gregory Bilotto.)

An interior view of the pedestrian bridge reveals a wide space afforded to passengers, likely for use of baggage carts. (Photograph by Gregory Bilotto.)

Newburgh's West Shore Railway Station, shown in several photographs from 2016, was built in 1909. The station, designed in the Beaux-Arts style, included numerous French details such as engaged columns, floral plasterwork, a large pediment, and carved elements within the pediment. Newburgh's railroad station corresponds with a group of five similar stations—in Mount Vernon, Poughkeepsie, Yonkers, and the since demolished station in White Plains. (Photograph by Gregory Bilotto.)

A closer view of the station's decorative pediment reveals the New York Central Railroad (abbreviated as NYCR or NYC after the NYCHRR merged in 1914) monogram emblazoned on a crest. Scrolling vines appear from Greek-styled vases, and throughout are acorns and oak leaves, powerful symbolic imagery of the Vanderbilt family. (Photograph by Gregory Bilotto.)

A rear view of the railroad station, facing the tracks, shows the lower-level baggage doors and a large second-story window that appears modern. The window was originally a set of doors that opened to a grand staircase allowing passengers to reach the tracks below. The facade was laid in red brick and secured with a Flemish bond; the brickwork alternated in patterns including the herringbone style. The roof was covered in red terra-cotta tiles of the Spanish Colonial Revival style. (Photograph by Gregory Bilotto.)

The 1910-built station for Hastings-on-Hudson, viewed from the entry facade, remains very well preserved. The station's plan has not deviated from the original, and many of its architectural details and interior furniture have been retained. The next several 2016 photographs reveal various features of the Beaux-Arts–style station. (Photograph by Gregory Bilotto.)

The facade of the station consists of ornamental red and brown brickwork in Flemish bond with various decorative patterns. Details of an elaborate geometric pattern from the entry facade are shown in the photograph. The eaves indicate the roof was built of wood and then covered with red terra-cotta tiles in the Spanish Colonial Revival style. (Photograph by Gregory Bilotto.)

The original hardwood door with brass fittings, when opened, permits passengers access to the pedestrian bridge and stairs reaching the platforms below. The triple bars at the base of the glass pane, called a triple push-bar, protected the glass from exiting baggage carts. Since glass panes run the length of the door, it is in the French style. (Photograph by Gregory Bilotto.)

The original brass light fixtures would have been electrified from power generated at the nearby Yonkers powerhouse. The chandelier has 12 bulbs resting in floral sockets that are attached to a ring. The ring is adorned with the acorn and oak leaves. The chandelier is centrally suspended in the waiting room. (Photograph by Gregory Bilotto.)

A brass sconce adorned with floral motifs and crowned with an acorn is one of a pair at the station. The lighting scheme provided illumination for hardwood benches in the waiting room. The sconces and benches with rounded seating and ends match examples in Grand Central Terminal and other suburban stations. (Photograph by Gregory Bilotto.)

An exterior view of the pedestrian bridge at the station shows riveted-steel construction and panes of glass windows running the length of the bridge. Although some sections have been repaired with modern materials, the bridge fits the typical design developed by the Associated Architects for the suburban station program. (Photograph by Gregory Bilotto.)

An exterior view of the station house from the pedestrian bridge reveals some of the ornate details, including corbels, knobs, and traces of French influences in the lower cornicing. A chimney from the interior fireplace and the support remnants of a baggage walkway are also visible. The platform's sealed doors and windows once connected to baggage services. (Photograph by Gregory Bilotto.)

The baggage elevator tower at the station is obsolete, and the baggage walkway connecting the tower and station house has been removed. Elements of the ornate decoration, however, are still visible in the brickwork and cornicing. The tower is representative of a time when the railroad was the principle form of overland transportation, even if traveling with several pieces of baggage. Whereas today, private motorcars have replaced this role. (Photograph by Gregory Bilotto.)

Another view from the pedestrian bridge looks down on the original cobbled roadway. The station was built along tracks running parallel to the Hudson River, thus the Hudson River Railroad in the NYCHRR. Ships sailing the river would arrive at docks adjacent to the various railroad stations to off-load passengers and goods. Excess ballast from these ships consisting of cobblestones would sometimes be discarded. These stones were then recycled into the roadways close to the waterfront. (Photograph by Gregory Bilotto.)

In 1911, the NYCHRR constructed Yonkers' main railroad station. Perhaps the most heavily used suburban station after opening, it was certainly the most ornate. A view of the grand entry facade, which was similar in plan to other stations in the group of five, has unique features, including a large window with a central clock, two ornate side windows, and a lavish pediment in the Beaux-Arts style. The next several 2015 photographs show the Yonkers station. (Photograph by Gregory Bilotto.)

In a closer view of the entry facade, intricate geometric patterns composed of tiles and red bricks complement the exterior. The elaborately carved pediment is framed with rows of floral motifs and dentiled cornicing, which is repeated around the arched window and along the facade below the eaves. An empty heraldic shield once held the NYCR monogram, while symbols of the Vanderbilt crest intertwine the borders and other details. The original roof cover did not survive and likely consisted of red terra-cotta tiles in the Spanish Colonial Revival style. (Photograph by Gregory Bilotto.)

A large domed hall provides access to the concourse, ticket windows, and a comfortable waiting room. Red brick in Flemish bond and French-inspired details form the walls, while the dome and pendentives are sheathed in sublime Guastavino tiles. Suspended from the dome's center, a brass chandelier with numerous globe-shaped bulbs, acorns, and oak leaves is a diminutive version of the type in the waiting room and main concourse at Grand Central Terminal. (Photograph by Gregory Bilotto.)

The station's ticket office on the right side of the domed entry hall is capped with an enormous clock. Engaged columns of red brick in Flemish bond are crowned with terra-cotta capitals. The capitals were emblazoned with the NYCR monogram and framed with the Vanderbilt acorns and oak leaves. The lamps above each ticket window and the doorway are nearly identical to those at Grand Central Terminal. (Photograph by Gregory Bilotto.)

On the left, within the station's domed hall, is the waiting room. Ornate wrought-iron gates spaced with columns of red brick separate the main hall from the waiting room. French architectural details frame the walls, and Tennessee pink marble runs the perimeter of the floors. The wrought-iron pattern is related to those on the exterior windows of the terminal's south facade. (Photograph by Gregory Bilotto.)

The high-ceilinged waiting room contains hardwood benches with rounded seating and ends, similar to the established decorative program. Above, arched windows illuminate the entire room, while the walls of red brick in Flemish bond meet tracery with floral motifs and geometric-patterned tiles. Double radiators, original to the period, provided heating during the colder months. Although unseen in the image, the roof rafters were constructed in walnut. (Photograph by Gregory Bilotto.)

A detail of a terra-cotta capital shows the NYCR monogram and the Vanderbilt acorns and oak leaves. A 2001–2004 restoration project, initiated through the railroad, cost $93,000,000. Several suburban railroad stations were returned to their original design, and the cost for Yonkers' station was $43,000,000. This funding paid for a California-based firm to specifically restore the station's intricate terra-cotta and other architectural details. (Photograph by Gregory Bilotto.)

A doorway indicating the telegraph office still remains in the station—the last vestige for an outmoded means of communication. Although these Gilded Age stations reflected the power and competitiveness of the NYCHRR and the Vanderbilts, unlike their lavish homes, these stations benefitted public service, offering a luxurious respite during travel. (Photograph by Gregory Bilotto.)

This view shows the domed ceiling done in a herringbone pattern with Guastavino tiles and framed by carved tracery. The floral-patterned tracery intertwined with the Vanderbilt acorns and oak leaves forms a repetitive pattern giving the impression of uninterrupted movement. (Photograph by Gregory Bilotto.)

Further details on the domed ceiling reveal interconnected bands and patterns of red brick in Flemish bond and Guastavino tiling. The NYCHRR and the Vanderbilt family exerted enormous architectural and artistic efforts to impress upon the passengers and rival railroad companies their prestige and dominance. (Photograph by Gregory Bilotto.)

Built in the Beaux-Arts style similar to the group of five, the Mount Vernon West station was constructed in 1914 but is now in disrepair. Years of ramshackle additions have preserved few details from the original design. Dissimilar to other suburban stations that hold firm to their original integrity or are modernized entirely, this station is a combination of both. The NYCR name framed above the front entry, the facade of red brick in Flemish bond, and French-styled cornicing are some of the few original details photographed in 2015. (Photograph by Gregory Bilotto.)

Hyde Park station was built in 1914 adjacent to the estate of Frederick William Vanderbilt (1856–1938), a grandson of Cornelius Vanderbilt. The lavish Vanderbilt home, constructed from 1896 to 1899, was designed in the Beaux-Arts style by McKim, Mead & White, while the one-story station was completed in the Mission Revival style. The Vanderbilt family paid the station's construction costs; however, they never used the station. Instead, the Vanderbilts arrived at Hyde Park via chauffeured motorcar. The Vanderbilts rarely traveled the railroad and if necessary arrived at the Poughkeepsie station. The station photographs were taken in 2015. (Photograph by Gregory Bilotto.)

The station contained waiting and baggage rooms with two fireplaces. The exterior was built with red brick in Flemish bond, while the roof was covered with red terra-cotta tiles in the Spanish Colonial Revival style. The large arched windows provide views of the Hudson River and Hudson Highlands Mountains. The exterior sign indicates the station is 79 miles from the platform at Grand Central Terminal and 361 miles from Buffalo. (Photograph by Gregory Bilotto.)

This is a view of the original baggage entry at the station, which opened to the at-grade platform. This detail was restored by the Hudson Valley Railroad Society, the organization responsible for maintaining and operating the station. The society also promotes the history of the NYCR and station. (Photograph by Gregory Bilotto.)

The 1914-built Rhinecliff station was designed in a version of the Mission Revival style. The exterior is devoid of most decoration but retains some French influence. These details include tan brickwork in Flemish bond, carved stones, cornicing, and corbels below the eaves. The roof is covered with red terra-cotta tiles in the Spanish Colonial Revival style. The arched fenestration has whitewashed framing, not an original feature. The station was photographed in 2016. (Photograph by Gregory Bilotto.)

The interior of the station, also with limited decoration, consists of tan brickwork in Flemish bond, while chandeliers with globe-shaped lamps are suspended from the ceiling. The ticket window, station furniture, and bench seating are original and match the established building program. (Photograph by Gregory Bilotto.)

In 1915, a railroad station was constructed for Hartsdale in the Tudor Revival style, similar to the Scarsdale station. The exterior was built with exposed timber beams and stucco, while the roof was covered in slate tiles. The interior, mostly whitewashed, retains few original details, except for a chandelier, ticket window with brass grille, and other exposed architectural elements typical of the style. Both photographs were taken in 2015. (Photograph by Gregory Bilotto.)

A closer view of the station's slate tiled roof reveals architectural details including crowning finials on either side of the gables and snow guards along the upper side of the eaves. The fan-shaped snow guards were used to protect passengers from any falling snow or ice, as the roof surface is smooth and accumulated snow and ice will not remain stable. (Photograph by Gregory Bilotto.)

Postmarked July 31, 1933, this mid-1930s Artvue Postcard Company real-photo postcard shows the 1916-built Bronxville railroad station. Written on the undivided back are details of a couple's return to Bronxville from a Philadelphia trip. Firefighting apparatus can be seen in the foreground, while the 1905-built Hotel Gramatan can be seen in the distance. (Collection of Gregory Bilotto.)

The Bronxville station's front entry shows a faithful interpretation in the Mission Revival style. The style was popularized in America, especially for railroad stations, during the late 19th and early 20th centuries. The origin was the Spanish Colonial missions built in California during the 17th and 18th centuries and reinvigorated through the Spanish Colonial Revival and Mission Revival styles. The station has curved gables, a long arcade, limited fenestration, and walls almost void of decoration or patterns, common features of the style. This and the other station photographs were taken in 2016. (Photograph by Gregory Bilotto.)

The roof was covered in red terra-cotta tiles in the Mission Revival style, while the upper windows were framed with a shell design. The minimalist capitals have a floral motif, with an almost hidden Vanderbilt acorn and oak leaf pattern. The interior retains original furniture, including benches with rounded seating and ends. (Photograph by Gregory Bilotto.)

A detail of the exterior ticket office window, covered with a cast-iron grille, shows heraldic imagery. Although designed in the Mission Revival style to complement the former Hotel Gramatan, an enormous and luxurious hotel built in the same style, hints of French influence appear. The caduceus and winged helmet are symbols of the Roman god Mercury, guardian of transportation and swiftness, and were popularized with the classicizing Beaux-Arts style. Appearing on the facade, they represent the railroad's speed. The hotel was razed in 1972, with only its arcade and elevator remaining today. (Photograph by Gregory Bilotto.)

This is a view of the pedestrian underpass, which facilitated passengers crossing the tracks below-grade, a design improvement from the Associated Architects and in keeping with the Mission Revival style. The passage was illuminated with windows running the length of the rise. (Photograph by Gregory Bilotto.)

A final detail from the station shows the original wooden and riveted-steel baggage entrance canopy. Although not a part of the style, practicality triumphed, and the baggage canopy was built to protect passengers and their effects. The lighting scheme and baggage door are original, though not in view. (Photograph by Gregory Bilotto.)

The 1918-built Poughkeepsie railroad station was one of the largest stations in the Hudson River Valley designed by the Associated Architects. Completed over five years in the Beaux-Arts style, it had 12 large arched windows and a high-ceilinged interior. The roof was covered in red terracotta tiles in the Spanish Colonial Revival style, while the facade consisted of red brick in Flemish bond. The next several photographs were taken in 2015. (Photograph by Gregory Bilotto.)

A closer view of the French architectural details reveals rosettes between each arched fenestration, bands of dentiled cornicing, acanthus corbels separated with smaller rosettes, and the Vanderbilt acorns and oak leaves intertwined throughout. The NYCR name appears, although a modern replacement. (Photograph by Gregory Bilotto.)

The station interior consists of a large waiting room, modeled after the same room at Grand Central Terminal. The high ceiling has exposed walnut rafters resting on interspersed corbels, while a fleur-de-lis border is repeated. There are 14 rows of chestnut benches lit with individual tray lamps. The large arched windows provide illumination during the day hours, and at night, the three original chandeliers, like those at the terminal, provide a comfortable glow. Unfortunately, several of the arched windows have been bricked closed. (Photograph by Gregory Bilotto.)

Examination of the station's benches and lighting proves their design is identical to the benches and lighting scheme of the main waiting room at Grand Central Terminal, which was completed only five years before Poughkeepsie's station. Similar to the terminal's designs, a border in Tennessee pink marble runs the perimeter of the station's floors. (Photograph by Gregory Bilotto.)

A reconstructed chandelier with original rosettes and acanthus leaves hangs from the walkway between the waiting room and pedestrian bridge at the station. A Vanderbilt acorn crown is likely missing. (Photograph by Gregory Bilotto.)

An exterior view of the baggage and goods loading dock shows three separate sets of doors with canopies as Poughkeepsie accommodated higher volumes of freight than most other stations. (Photograph by Gregory Bilotto.)

The original at-grade platform and the riveted-steel and green-painted walkway both run from the station house to the adjacent Main Street bridge. The walkway still connects the station with Main Street businesses. The riveted-steel pedestrian bridge, painted green, can be seen in the distance. (Photograph by Gregory Bilotto.)

A riveted-steel staircase, painted green, still provides passengers access to the platforms from the Main Street businesses above. Glass panes run the length of the stairs. The original covered walkway leading from the station to Main Street is visible, but the upper section of the attached pavilion is a modern reproduction. (Photograph by Gregory Bilotto.)

The Fordham station was rebuilt between 1909 and 1918, as part of the Grand Central Terminal building program. The station shows details in the Beaux-Arts style including an exterior of red brick in Flemish bond, arched windows, carved-stone highlights, and red terra-cotta tiled roof in the Spanish Colonial Revival style. The NYCR name is noted in tiles above the entrance. The station is pictured in 2016. (Photograph by Gregory Bilotto.)

The interior of the station is unlike any of the suburban stations built by the Associated Architects. The waiting room is small and almost unusable, consisting of solitary bench seating, although similar to other suburban station furniture. Multiple globe-shaped lamps provide illumination, and the ticket office extends into the waiting room occupying a large area. It seems the station was modified but retained numerous elements from the original 19th-century structure. (Photograph by Gregory Bilotto.)

The French-influenced Glenwood railroad station was constructed between 1909 and 1918, providing rail access to another segment of Yonkers. The station is situated close to the powerhouse, which once generated electricity for the railroad and powered the same station. The powerhouse's twin smokestacks can be seen in the distance. The view along Glenwood Avenue looking toward the station was taken in 2015. (Photograph by Gregory Bilotto.)

A closer view of the station shows a facade with red brick in Flemish bond, tiles laid in a geometric pattern, carved-stone details, French-style hardwood doors, and red terra-cotta tiles in the Spanish Colonial Revival style. A riveted-steel pedestrian bridge and stairs, painted green, carry passengers from the station to the platform. These are original to the station but are not in view; the lighting scheme is modern. (Photograph by Gregory Bilotto.)

This 2015 photograph and the following image show the ruined Yonkers powerhouse. The powerhouse was designed in the Beaux-Arts style, and with no public access intended, the elaborate decorative details added to the structure are astonishing. The exterior was built with red bricks in Flemish bond, laid in dentiled and segmented patterns at the roofline. Numerous arched windows pierce the facade, allowing natural light. This structure once housed boilers and turbines. (Photograph by Gregory Bilotto.)

The roof of the boiler and turbine structure was covered with glass, allowing further light to penetrate the large interior space. The roof gables were assembled with riveted-steel beams, and the intermediate space was filled with glass panes, creating a Tudor Revival–style design. The demolished Port Morris powerhouse was constructed with similar architectural details. (Photograph by Gregory Bilotto.)

The cavernous interior of the boiler and turbine room indicates the quantity of steam needed to generate electric power for the rail lines and stations. At the base of the tri-arched windows is a large coal chute. Coal was unloaded from freight trains and fueled the boilers, generating steam. The steam pushed the turbines. A coal store was located in a smaller structure at the waterfront and coal arrived via ship on the Hudson River. Coal transport via rail was likely a secondary source used during the winter months, while the river was unnavigable. (Photograph by Gregory Bilotto.)

The Port Morris powerhouse was located in the Port Morris section of Bronx County. An interior view taken on September 24, 1906, reveals the boiler and turbine room with four large boilers several stories in height and equally large turbines. This power equipment would have been identical to that in the former Yonkers powerhouse. This photograph was taken by a NYCHRR photographer. (Courtesy of the NYCHRR Archives in the NYPL Irma and Paul Milstein Division of United States History, Local History, and Genealogy).

The exterior facade of the two-story substation shows elaborate brickwork and arched window construction. Remnants of the lighting scheme are visible between each window in this 2015 image. (Photograph by Gregory Bilotto.)

The substation's grand entry shows French details with acanthus corbels supporting a classical pediment in this 2015 image. The NYCR monogram is emblazoned within the pediment and framed with two decorative elements displaying the Vanderbilt acorns and oak leaves. This ornate ornamentation is highly unusual since it was unlikely any Vanderbilt visited the powerhouse and it was a nonpublic space. The extreme competition between the rival railroad companies probably spurred such embellishment on nonpublic buildings. (Photograph by Gregory Bilotto.)

The large converters on the first floor of the building were designed by the General Electric Company. The steam produced from the coal-burning boilers and turbines would generate alternating current, or AC. These rotary converters would then convert the AC to direct current, or DC. DC power was then stored in large batteries. This and the next three images were taken in 2015. (Photograph by Gregory Bilotto.)

A bridge connects the boiler and turbine structure with the substation's second floor. The ornate riveted-steel lampposts show incredible detail, again unusual for a nonpublic space. (Photograph by Gregory Bilotto.)

The transmission pole once carried electric lines along the tracks to power the Glenwood station. Made from riveted steel, the ornate design has aesthetic details. It became too expensive for the NYCR to produce electricity, and operations were assumed by the New York Edison Company (now Consolidated Edison, Inc.). As more economical methods for generating electricity were developed, the powerhouses were eventually shuttered. (Photograph by Gregory Bilotto.)

Several heaps of monochrome glazed bricks were found around the powerhouse buildings. These dark-purple bricks stamped with a floral pattern once covered the floor of the substation. (Photograph by Gregory Bilotto.)

A NYCHRR photograph from September 25, 1906, the year of electrification, shows the French-styled Kingsbridge substation in the Kingsbridge section of Bronx County. Although the railroad employed DC power, the current was unstable and could not be transported long distance. Substations were built to essentially boost DC power, which was stored in large batteries. (Courtesy of the NYCHRR Archives in the NYPL Irma and Paul Milstein Division of United States History, Local History, and Genealogy).

The Kingsbridge substation, as photographed in 2016, is nearly identical to the Yonkers substation. It was closed after power production methods changed and is now derelict. Many of the French architectural details are, however, still visible, including the brickwork in Flemish bond, laid in dentiled and segmented patterns. The signal tower situated on the north side of the building has since been razed. (Photograph by Gregory Bilotto.)

This NYCHRR photograph, taken on July 18, 1906, shows the interior of the Kingsbridge substation's power storage room. These batteries boosted DC power generated from the Yonkers and Port Morris powerhouses. The image reveals the same monochrome glazed bricks found at the Yonkers powerhouse. (Courtesy of the NYCHRR Archives in the NYPL Irma and Paul Milstein Division of United States History, Local History, and Genealogy).

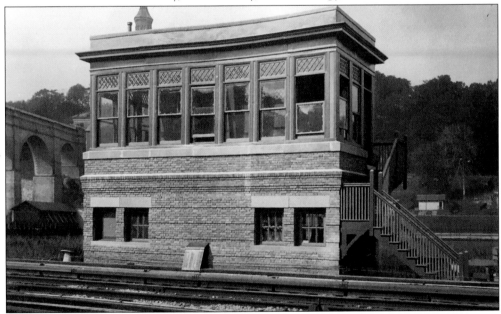

The High Bridge signal tower functioned as a control center, alerting approaching trains and operating switches. The building reflected French influences, with segmented brickwork in Flemish bond, large cornicing, lintels, and glass tracery. These towers, constructed along the railroad, became obsolete when functions were automated through a centralized control center. The majority of the towers were then demolished, including at the High Bridge. This photograph was taken by a NYCHRR photographer during the electrification process. (Courtesy of the NYCHRR Archives in the NYPL Irma and Paul Milstein Division of United States History, Local History, and Genealogy).

A NYCHRR photograph, dated July 12, 1906, shows below-grade track in the Port Morris area. Above the track is a view of sparse development in Port Morris, consisting of two solitary mid-19th century buildings set in the natural terrain. Seven years before the opening of Grand Central Terminal, parts of Bronx County were considered hinterland. (Courtesy of the NYCHRR Archives in the NYPL Irma and Paul Milstein Division of United States History, Local History, and Genealogy).

A second photograph with the same date provides a view into the Port Morris area of Bronx County. The below-grade track has cut a swathe through the natural terrain separating a tenement house from a distant farm. Two pedestrian bridges spanning the track have modified stairs at either end, comprised of wooden planks. Outside the tenement, clotheslines hang across the yard, and an outhouse is visible in the foreground. (Courtesy of the NYCHRR Archives in the NYPL Irma and Paul Milstein Division of United States History, Local History, and Genealogy).

Five

LATER YEARS, RENAISSANCE, AND MODERN DAY

After the Second World War and with construction of the Dwight D. Eisenhower National System of Interstate and Defense Highways, newly manufactured cars would be catapulted to the primary mode of transportation. This had disastrous consequences for railroads, especially Grand Central Terminal, as they faded into obsolescence, culminating with destruction of the temple to transportation, Pennsylvania Station. It was razed and carted away as New Jersey landfill in the 1960s. The wrecking ball next moved to Grand Central Terminal. Bankrupt and without any hope for renovation, it had become a filthy eyesore obscuring Park Avenue, with a significant population of disadvantaged New Yorkers living within. Then, former first lady Jacqueline Kennedy Onassis (1929–1994) arrived and worked tirelessly to protect the once grand terminal from total destruction through a network of grassroots support for the historic preservation of architecture.

In 1968, the financially struggling NYCR merged with its longtime rival, the Pennsylvania Railroad, forming the Pennsylvania Central Transportation Company (Penn Central). Penn Central entered insolvency in 1970 and, through a 1976 act of Congress, was nationalized, creating the Consolidated Rail Corporation (Conrail). The end had come for private ownership of railroads; once the most powerful American company directed by the richest family in America, the NYCR had been consumed and vanished into history. The Metropolitan Transportation Authority (MTA), another 1960s creation, assumed control of the Conrail commuter railroad network in 1983, forming the Metro-North Commuter Railroad (Metro-North), which currently operates the suburban railroad network and stations. In 1994, the MTA began a restoration project, returning the almost derelict terminal to the grandeur it held on opening day. Every aspect of the terminal was transformed— from cracks to new stones and even the constellation ceiling.

Grand Central Terminal has today reclaimed its glorious past, as the structure has adapted to meet the ever-changing needs of the modern traveler. The increased congestion and pollution from cars and the awareness of climate change have projected the terminal into a realm of importance. An additional benefit remains the original concept of William John Wilgus's air rights, which had a major role in the terminal's renaissance. The continual construction of skyscrapers in the area around the terminal has led to an increased use of the terminal, infrastructure upgrades, and increased public awareness of the terminal's importance. The recent construction of supertall skyscrapers, however, has generated negative effects. The historic view of Grand Central Terminal, the temple of transport, has been erased, replaced with what many consider elitism, exclusivity, and an image of ostentatious wealth similar to that perpetuated during the Gilded Age.

In this view looking north on the Park Avenue Viaduct, the majestic terminal fills the horizon, like the rising sun, in a photograph from the 1930s–1940s. Whitney Warren's vision of the terminal based upon medieval French design, with cathedrals the central point of a city, has been realized. The NYCR Building, by the same architect and firm, radiates above the terminal resembling the tower of a Gothic cathedral. A cathedral's portal sculpture, the dominant element with Christ enthroned or crucified, has found symmetry in the dramatic sculpture of Jules-Félix Coutan and the mammoth clock by Louis Comfort Tiffany. (Collection of Gregory Bilotto.)

The 1884-built Murray Hill Hotel at the edge of the Murray Hill zone and once adjacent to Grand Central Depot, is shown in this image datable to the 1930s. The Victorian building, which had been open for business through all three phases of railroad properties, would be razed in the late 1940s. The hotel had a colorful history and survived a fire and even a wave of robberies during the Depression, when a cat burglar targeted the jewelry of rich guests and residents. The terminal and NYCR Building are visible in the distance. (Photograph by Berenice Abbott, courtesy of the Changing New York Collection in the NYPL Miriam and Ira D. Wallach Division of Art, Prints, and Photographs.)

The next several photographs were taken in 1941 by photographers documenting scenes for the US government. Passengers were photographed passing through the terminal two months before American entry into the Second World War. The windows of the terminal would be painted black, to deflect detection by German submarines. The majority of this paint would not be removed from the fenestrations until the 1994 MTA restoration. (Negative by John Collier, courtesy of the Farm Security Administration and Office of War Information Black-and-White Negatives Collection in the LOC Prints and Photographs Division.)

A second view from the same date shows passengers in the main concourse. Years of tobacco smoking in the terminal would stain the walls and ceilings black, matching the painted windows and also not removed until the MTA restoration. (Negative by John Collier, courtesy of the Farm Security Administration and Office of War Information Black-and-White Negatives Collection in the LOC Prints and Photographs Division.)

Photographer Milton Tinsley is working on a model in the Visual Unit of the Farm Security Administration. The model represents a photomural destined for the terminal. Created in 1935, the Farm Security Administration was a product of the New Deal. The reformist photography staff documented the plight of the Great Depression. (Negative by John Collier, courtesy of the Farm Security Administration and Office of War Information Black-and-White Negatives Collection in the LOC Prints and Photographs Division.)

Milton Tinsley is again shown working on a model for the photomural. The Farm Security Administration's role became dishonorable with the outbreak of the Second World War. The agency was responsible for the seizure and redistribution of private farms owned by American citizens of Japanese descent. (Negative by John Collier, courtesy of the Farm Security Administration and Office of War Information Black-and-White Negatives Collection in the LOC Prints and Photographs Division.)

The terminal would play a similar role during the Second World War as it did during the first. The US government produced the photomural as wartime propaganda and collected funds in support of the war effort. Grand Central Terminal was selected as large volumes of passengers and entire regiments of soldiers passed through its concourse. (Negative by Arthur Rothstein, courtesy of the Farm Security Administration and Office of War Information Black-and-White Negatives Collection in the LOC Prints and Photographs Division.)

In the early 1950s, cars were in full production and the railroad was bleeding money, leading to major financial problems by the 1960s and eventual bankruptcy in the 1970s. Ironically, a 1955 Oldsmobile Rocket 88 is shown in the terminal's concourse. Perhaps unknown to the NYCR at the time, the motorcar was the primary cause for its misfortune. (Collection of Gregory Bilotto.)

With a view looking south on Vanderbilt Avenue toward East Forty-Second Street and Pershing Square, this 2016 photograph is similar to one taken during construction of the subterranean railyard. The railroad's annex has been replaced with the MetLife Building (formerly Pan Am Building), built between 1960 and 1963 in the International Style. Penn Central's bankruptcy in the 1960s gave architect Marcel Lajos Breuer (1902–1981) an opportunity to propose a 55-story office tower, to be built over the terminal in an effort to generate revenue. (Photograph by Gregory Bilotto.)

Classicism meets modernism—Grand Central Terminal and the MetLife Building are viewed from Vanderbilt Avenue. The 2016 view might have been different with Marcel Lajos Breuer's tower, if not for creation of the Landmarks Preservation Commission. The terminal, listed with the commission, was therefore entitled to legal protection from alteration or demolition. Penn Central and its real property interests fought a legal battle with preservationists reaching the Supreme Court. In *Penn Central Transportation Company v. New York City*, the court protected the terminal's landmark status in 1978. (Photograph by Gregory Bilotto.)

The Sterling Bronze Company created the magnificent chandeliers in the main concourse and waiting room, as shown in this 2016 image. The lighting scheme design and ornamentation are in the Beaux-Arts style, consisting mostly of elaborate French floral decorations and Vanderbilt acorns with oak leaves. Devised during the MTA restoration, all the lighting was restored and reproductions were true to the original design. From 1927 to 1998, the rise below the chandeliers was covered with ticket offices, creating a dark passage. The rise was reopened and returned to the original design. (Photograph by Gregory Bilotto.)

This image, datable to 1980–2006, shows the information desk clock, a priceless self-winding timepiece fabricated by the Self Winding Clock Company in Brooklyn. The globe-shaped brass clock has four illuminated faces, each covered in opaline glass, and is crowned with the Vanderbilt acorn. Below the clock, a spiral staircase connects the information desk with a companion desk directly underneath on the suburban concourse. (Photograph by Carol M. Highsmith, courtesy of the Carol M. Highsmith Archive in the Library of Congress Prints and Photographs Division.)

Perhaps the ultimate example of the Vanderbilt family, above each track entry on the suburban concourse is an oak tree branch that twists around a trellis interspersed with oak leaves and acorns. The trellis is pinned with rosettes and illuminated with a solitary lamp in this 2016 image. The French sculptor Sylvain Salières (1865–1920) carved the crest in Tennessee pink marble and was responsible for the decorative program at the terminal. During the MTA restoration, the original Tennessee quarry was located and reopened. Blocks of stone were then carted off for repairs at the terminal. (Photograph by Gregory Bilotto.)

A hidden tunnel into Grand Central Terminal adorned in Guastavino tiling was photographed in 2016. Taxis once drove the two-direction carriageway, dropping and receiving passengers at the terminal, which can still be accessed at East Forty-Fourth Street below the former Commodore Hotel. (Photograph by Gregory Bilotto.)

A 2016 view through Grand Central Terminal's enormous arched windows shows an image of the fourth-floor walkway passing through the south facade. The terminal has four halls with six stories, and connecting the halls and floors on the north and south sides are several walkways through glass windows. The walkways are illuminated and provide access to the various offices, mechanical rooms, and storage on either side, including the Frederick Ely Williamson Library and Archives. The walkways also provide for the terminal's great windows to be cranked open, allowing cool air to enter before central air-conditioning was installed. (Photograph by Gregory Bilotto.)

A second 2016 view from the same fourth-floor walkway shows the floor above. The walkway's floors were made of two-inch-thick cut-rock crystal. It was reported that the weight of the glass needed to support several walkways within the windows would be too great. Rock crystal is exceptionally light in weight. (Photograph by Gregory Bilotto.)

The 1869 bronze statue of Cornelius Vanderbilt originally graced the facade of the Hudson River Railroad freight depot in St. John's Park. After completion of the terminal, it was relocated from the depot, likely after it was razed, to the base of the south facade's central window, just steps from the former Commodore Hotel entrance on the Park Avenue Viaduct, as shown in this 2016 image. (Photograph by Gregory Bilotto.)

The next several images from 2016 show various Grand Central Terminal landmarks, revealing preservation or loss since construction began in 1903. Looking south, Whitney Warren's Francophile view of Grand Central Terminal as Park Avenue's apex is lost. Skyscrapers have a stranglehold over the terminal. Beside the NYCR Building and the MetLife Building, the left is dominated by 245 Park Avenue. The 1967-built glass skyscraper occupies the former site of the glamorous Grand Central Palace, which opened on Lexington Avenue. (Photograph by Gregory Bilotto.)

The Biltmore Hotel, once a part of the grand trio of luxury hotels that surrounded the terminal, has been radically transformed. Known today as Bank of America Plaza, or 335 Madison Avenue, it was stripped to the steel structural framing and sheathed in glass and red granite between 1981 and 1983. Despite having landmark preservation status and with active protesters in the street in a vain attempt at salvation, it was lost and only the original building outline remains today. (Photograph by Gregory Bilotto.)

The Commodore Hotel (now Grand Hyatt Hotel) helped form the grand trio of the terminal's hotels. The lower floors were ruthlessly stripped to the steel structural framing from 1976 to 1980 by the Trump Organization, and a glass facade was attached to the remaining masonry facade, a construction variation from the former Biltmore Hotel. The new building retains the original outline from Warren & Wetmore's 1919 hotel. The view from East Forty-Second Street shows the majestic Chrysler Building at right and the MetLife Building reflected in the hotel's shimmering windows. (Photograph by Gregory Bilotto.)

In 1923, the Pershing Square Building, built in the Romanesque Revival style, opened over the former Grand Union Hotel. It was named after the Great War hero and General of the Armies John Joseph Pershing (1860–1948); he was the first American general awarded a sixth star by Congress (the other being a posthumous award to Pres. George Washington). The Park Avenue Viaduct, which passes over the square below, was also named after the general. Visible in the lower right is one of two original cast-iron eagles presented to the terminal. (Photograph by Gregory Bilotto.)

666 Fifth Avenue, built in 1957 and clad in aluminium panels, replaced the William Kissam Vanderbilt home. As the avenue became highly commercialized, the 14 Vanderbilt family homes once located in Midtown were nearly all demolished. In this view looking north on Fifth Avenue, similar to a stereoscopic view from 1903, the twin churches remain. Both are draped in black safety netting during restoration. (Photograph by Gregory Bilotto.)

After opening in 1928, Edwin Goodman's (1876?–1953) Beaux-Arts department store Bergdorf Goodman epitomized commercial development on Fifth Avenue. The Plaza Hotel at right, in the Châteauesque style, is almost a mirror image of the Manhattan Hotel. Both buildings were completed by the architect Henry Janeway Hardenbergh. The Plaza Hotel is one of the few remaining Gilded Age hotels. (Photograph by Gregory Bilotto.)

The Crown Building survives from the 1920s, when commercialization on Fifth Avenue was rampant. Warren & Wetmore's high-rise was built with architectural details in the French Renaissance style, including the 416-foot-high gilt crown at its apex. The crown was illuminated regally at night, located above an octagonal tower with dormers, parapets, terra-cotta details, and other features are all in common with the French style. An original weather vane, the pinnacle of the crown, was seized in 1942 for the war effort. In the 1920s, jewellers and dealers sold Art Deco accoutrements in the building's galleries, and in 1929 the Museum of Modern Art opened in its first home, on the 12th floor. (Photograph by Gregory Bilotto.)

Artist John Fleming Gould (1906–1996) completed this original artwork of Grand Central Station and 1871 train shed to commemorate the railroad electrification in 1906. The older steam-powered locomotive remains behind in the shed, surpassed by the newly electrified train, propelling the railroad into the future. The mid-20th-century artwork presents the importance of electrification for both the railroad and the future of transportation. (Courtesy of the John Fleming Gould Collection in the Bethlehem Art Gallery.)

As several original terminal zone buildings were demolished to construct One Vanderbilt Avenue, this final view of Grand Central Terminal has been unseen for over 100 years. The supertall skyscraper is slated to become the second-tallest in New York City, but will likely be overtaken by others before completion. A 1902-built Warren & Wetmore office tower and the 1922-built Liggett Building by the firm Carrère & Hastings, among others, fell to the wrecking ball. The project was approved with financial incentives for social programs and public transport improvements, totalling $220,000,000. These massive constructions in glass are products of the new Gilded Age. (Photograph by Gregory Bilotto.)

BIBLIOGRAPHY

Belle, John, and Maxinne R. Leighton. *Grand Central: Gateway to a Million Lives*. New York: W.W. Norton, 2000.

Dunlap, David. "A Once Mysterious Stone Wall Holds a Link to a Rail Boom." *New York Times*, August 27, 2015.

Fellheimer, Alfred T., and Stem, Allen H. *Inception and Creation of Grand Central Terminal*. New York: n.p. 1913.

Finamore, Roy, and Sandy Ingbert. *The Grand Central Oyster Bar and Restaurant Cookbook: Recipes and Tales from a Classic American Restaurant*. New York: Stewart, Tabori, and Chang, 2013.

Fitch, James Marston, and Diana S. Waite. *Grand Central Terminal and Rockefeller Center: A Historic-Critical Estimate of their Significance*. Albany: New York State Parks and Recreation Division for Historic Preservation, 1974.

Klein, Aaron E. *New York Central*. New York: Smithmark Publishers, 1995.

Leavy, Michael. *The New York Central System*. Charleston, SC: Arcadia Publishing, 2006.

Middleton, William D. *Grand Central: The World's Greatest Railway Terminal*. San Marino, CA: Golden West Books, 1977.

Morrison, David D. *The Cast Iron Eagles of Grand Central Station*. Plainview, NY: Cannonball Publications, 1998.

New York Central & Hudson River Railroad Company: Plans of Grand Central Terminal During Construction Process and Architects/ Engineers Proposed Plans and Drawings. New York: New York Central & Hudson River Railroad, 1907.

New York Central Railroad Electric Zone: New York District. New York: New York Central & Hudson River Railroad, 1906.

New York Times. "Fifteen Killed in Rear End Collision: Train Crashes in Darkness of Park Avenue Tunnel." January 9, 1902.

Nevins, Deborah, ed. *Grand Central Terminal: City Within the City*. New York: The Municipal Art Society of New York, 1982.

Ochsendorf, John. *Guastavino Vaulting: The Art of the Structural Tile*. New York: Princeton Architectural Press, 2010.

Pennoyer, Peter, and Anne Walker. *The Architecture of Warren & Wetmore*. New York: W.W. Norton, 2006.

Rinaldi, Thomas E., and Robert J. Yasinsac. *Hudson Valley Ruins: Forgotten Landmarks of an American Landscape*. Lebanon, NH: University Press of New England, 2006.

Robert N. Dennis Collection of Stereoscopic Views, New York Public Library, Miriam and Ira D. Wallach Division of Art, Prints, and Photographs.

Robins, Anthony W., and the New York Transit Museum. *Grand Central Terminal: 100 Years of a New York Landmark*. New York: Stewart, Tabori and Chang, 2013.

Root, William Stanton. "A History of the Grand Central Station." *Railroad Man's Magazine*, November 1903.

Schlichting, Kurt C. *Grand Central Terminal: Railroads, Engineering, and Architecture in New York City*. Baltimore: John Hopkins University Press, 2001.

Souvenir and Official Programme of the Press Club Fair: Grand Central Palace. New York: Home Seeker Printing and Publishing Company, 1893.

Views of Grand Central Terminal: Photographs of the Architect's Drawings Showing the Proposed Appearance of the Terminal and its Surroundings. New York: New York Central & Hudson River Railroad, n.d.

Wilgus, William John. "Grand Central Terminal in Perspective." *Transactions of the American Society of Civil Engineers*, 106 (1941): 992–1051.

INDEX

Discover Thousands of Local History Books
Featuring Millions of Vintage Images

Arcadia Publishing, the leading local history publisher in the United States, is committed to making history accessible and meaningful through publishing books that celebrate and preserve the heritage of America's people and places.

Find more books like this at
www.arcadiapublishing.com

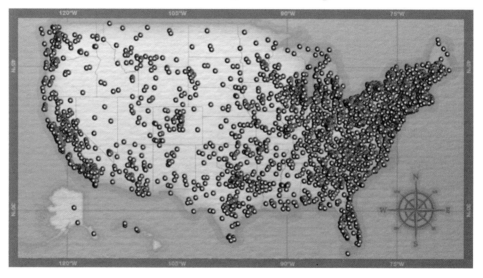

Search for your hometown history, your old stomping grounds, and even your favorite sports team.